FOR GRANDMAS WHO DO WINDOWS

THIRD EDITION
REVISED AND ENLARGED

2005

by

Amy C. Lowenstein

DITHRIDGE PRESS
PITTSBURGH PENNSYLVANIA

ISBN 0-9713054-2-0

TABLE OF CONTENTS

1. INTRODUCTION

2. LEARNING ABOUT WINDOWS

3. WORKING WITH FILES AND FOLDERS

4. CUSTOMIZING YOUR COMPUTER

5. WORKING WITH PICTURES

6. ADDRESS BOOK

7. COMPUTER CARE

8. E-MAIL

9. THE INTERNET AND THE WEB

INTRODUCTION TO WINDOWS

Chapter 1

ABOUT THIS MANUAL

The easiest books to use are cookbooks. There are no diagrams and very little conversation. For each recipe the ingredients are listed, followed by the instructions.

You don't have to know why you bake a cake at a particular temperature or understand how your oven works. All you need to know is how to set the temperature.

Using a computer is not much different than following a recipe. The biggest difference is that when you use a computer you must be precise. There is no such thing as adding an extra pinch of salt or substituting margarine for butter. Computers do have one major advantage - in most cases you can correct your mistakes easily.

Instructions for accessing the Internet in this manual are for those whose Internet server is America Online because it is one of the largest of the commercial online services. This edition is based on Windows XP Home Edition. Because basic concepts are the same in all the versions of Windows, this edition is essentially applicable to earlier versions of Windows.

STEP-BY-STEP INSTRUCTIONS

This manual is based on the same concept as a cookbook. There are no diagrams. Each topic includes a brief introduction followed by step-by-step instructions.

THE EASIEST WAYS

Just as there are many recipes for making the same item, Windows has many ways to do the same thing. Often, which way you choose depends upon which window you are working in. The methods chosen for this manual are, in most cases, the most direct and the easiest.

INSTRUCTIONS TO RESCUE YOU WHEN YOU GET INTO TROUBLE

Most beginning computer users have one thing in common - they make mistakes, throwing themselves into a state of instant confusion. Not only do new users make mistakes; they usually make the same mistakes.

What matters is not making a mistake, but when a mistake is made, knowing how to correct it. This manual recognizes that there are certain procedures where it is easy to go wrong. Wherever a mistake is likely to occur, a "Get Out of Trouble" box is provided that tells you how to correct your error.

READY REFERENCE

In addition to teaching computer basics, this manual has been designed for use as a quick reference tool. It is not necessary to remember everything. The user-friendly index makes it easy to find specific subjects.

YOUR COMPUTER IS JUST LIKE YOUR KITCHEN

Think of your computer as a kitchen. It is a place to cook with electrical outlets for all your appliances.

How powerful is your computer? It depends. If you purchased one with a lot of capability, you are using a food processor. If you bought one with minimum capability, you are using a hand-held beater.

A program is nothing more than a recipe. The only difference is that the computer does the work and you don't have any pots or pans to wash.

When you bake a cake, you need counter space. When your cake is done, you need storage space. It is the same thing with your computer. When it is running a program it needs working space. When the computer is finished with the program, it needs storage space.

If you want to put the cake away to serve some other time, you can put it in your freezer. If you have files that you want to use some other time, you can put them on a floppy disk.

THE CURSOR - NOT SOMEONE WHO SWEARS - ALTHOUGH YOU PROBABLY WILL!

Imagine standing in front of a blackboard with a long stick in your hand pointing to a spot in a sentence on the board where you want to insert a word. The cursor is that stick - a pointer in the form of a blinking vertical line that marks an insertion point. Whether you are at the beginning or in the middle of a sentence or word, the cursor must be positioned at the insertion point for you to be able to type.

As you move the mouse over the window screen, what looks like a capital "I" appears. It moves as you move the mouse. Place the "I" at the insertion point. Click the mouse. The blinking cursor appears, marking the insertion point.

To insert the cursor into existing text, it must always be positioned between two characters or words or at the beginning or end of a sentence or paragraph. It does not appear on top of a character.

Text that you type always appears to the left of the cursor. When you are finished typing, the cursor will continue to blink at the spot where you stopped until you exit the file or proceed to another function.

The arrows on the keyboard can also be used to move the blinking cursor. The Right and Left arrow keys move the cursor forward or backward one character at a time. The Up and Down arrow keys move the cursor up or down one line at a time.

Sometimes the blinking cursor appears automatically in a box in which you are to enter information. It is telling you to begin typing at that spot. If the cursor is not there, click on the box and the cursor will appear at the insertion point.

THE MOUSE - YOUR MOST IMPORTANT UTENSIL

You cannot do a thing with your computer until you have mastered using the mouse.

CLICKING

Place your hand on the mouse. The wire attached to the mouse faces the computer. Your index finger rests on the left button and your next finger on the right button. Using your index finger, press down once on the left-hand mouse button and release immediately. This is called clicking.

POINTING

The mouse is a pointing device. Turn on your computer. The Start Button appears in the lower left-hand corner of the screen. The Desktop icons are displayed. Put your hand on the mouse and move it around, keeping it flat on the surface of the mouse pad. You will see an arrow moving on your screen. Practice moving the arrow from icon to icon, but do not click.

DRAGGING

You can move an item from one place to another by keeping the left button depressed while moving the mouse to a new location. When you have reached the spot where you want to place the item, release the button. The item will be in its new location. This is called dragging and dropping.

SCROLLING

Between the left-hand and right-hand buttons on the mouse is a scroll button. Place your index finger on the scroll button. To move up a line on the screen, roll the scroll button upwards. To move down a line on the screen, roll the scroll button downwards.

THE RIGHT-HAND BUTTON

The right-hand button on the mouse is only used to activate special commands.

SOLITAIRE - PRACTICE MAKES PERFECT

An easy way to develop mouse skills is to play Solitaire on the computer.

❑   Turn on your computer.

❑   Move the mouse so that the arrow rests on the Start Button in the lower left-hand corner.

❑ Click on Start. The Start Menu appears on the screen. On the Start Menu is the word All Programs followed by an arrow.

GET INTO TROUBLE?

If you make a mistake such as clicking in the wrong place, don't worry! Move the mouse to a blank spot on the screen and click one time. You will be returned to the beginning. Computers don't wear out. You can keep starting over until you get it.

If you open a program by mistake, click on the Exit Button (the one with the X on it in the upper right-hand corner) to exit. You will be returned to where you started.

❑ Glide the mouse to the word All Programs. All Programs will be highlighted. A sub-menu appears. Locate the word Games in the sub-menu.

❑ Glide the mouse across All Programs.

❑ Glide the mouse upward to the word Games. Games will be highlighted. A sub-menu appears to the right.

DON'T GIVE UP!

Everybody goofs here - it may take several tries to get it right. When you position the mouse on All Programs, the sub-menu appears very quickly. If you move the mouse before you know where you are going, sub-menus will appear from all directions.

Click on a blank spot on Desktop, which is still visible. The Start Menu and all the sub-menus will disappear. You can now try again by clicking the Start Button.

Do not move the mouse from All Programs until you locate Games on the next menu. To move to Games, glide the mouse across All Programs and up to Games. Glide the mouse across Games and down to Solitaire.

❑ Glide the mouse over the word Games to the sub-menu and down to the word Solitaire.

❑ Click on Solitaire. The Solitaire game will appear on the screen. The game has already been dealt.

   In the right corner are four blank spaces. This is where you drag the aces and subsequent cards. You can also move the aces by double clicking on them. In the left corner is the stack of cards. When you click on the stack, the cards turn.

   When all the cards in the stack have been turned, click on the circle that appears on the left to turn the cards again.

Move the cards by dragging. Click on a card to turn it over. Continue playing until the game is finished.

❑   Click on Game on the Menu bar. A drop-down menu appears. To play again:

❑   Click on Deal. A new game will be dealt.

❑   To exit, click on the Exit Button in the upper right-hand corner (the one with the X on it). You are returned to Desktop.

The above instructions are provided for you to learn to use the mouse. If you want more detailed instructions on playing Solitaire:

❑   Click on Help on the Solitaire Menu Bar. A drop-down menu appears.

❑   Click on Contents. The Solitaire Help window appears. It contains a split screen.

❑   Click on Solitaire in the left-hand screen. A drop-down menu appears.

❑   Click on any option to select it.   Instructions for the option you selected appear in the scroll box on the right.

❑   Click on the down arrow in the scroll box to view all the text.

❑   Continue clicking any option on the left in order to view instructions which will appear on the right.

❑   Exit by clicking on the Exit Button in the upper right-hand corner of the Solitaire Help window (the one with the X on it).

❑   The program returns you to the Solitaire game window.

TURN ON YOUR COMPUTER AND RUN FOR HELP!

Some computers include an introductory program with the pre-installed software. Check your computer manual to see if one was included. If the program has been installed, there is probably an icon for it on Desktop. Double click the icon to open the program. The instructions are normally geared for beginners and will familiarize you with your computer.

Windows XP provides both a short introductory tutorial and the Microsoft Interactive Training Course for Windows XP Home Edition. There is also a Help and Support program which can be accessed at any time.

WINDOWS XP INTRODUCTORY TUTORIAL

❑ Click on Start. The Start Menu appears on the screen. On the Start Menu are the words "All Programs."

❑ Click on All Programs. All Programs will be highlighted. A sub-menu appears on the right.

❑ Glide the mouse across All Programs and up to the word Accessories.

❑ Click on Accessories.

❑ Glide the mouse across Accessories and down to Tour Windows XP. The Windows XP Tour window appears containing two options for displaying the tour. One provides for an animated tour with voice narration. The other provides a tour with text and images only.

❑ Click on the circle next to the option you wish to choose. A black dot appears in the circle.

❑ Click on the Next Button at the bottom of the window. The Windows XP Tour begins. Follow the instructions as they appear on the screen.

❑ Click on the red Exit Button (the one with an X on it) to exit. Desktop appears.

MICROSOFT INTERACTIVE TRAINING COURSE FOR WINDOWS XP HOME EDITION

❑ Click on Start. The Start Menu appears on the screen. On the Start Menu are the words "All Programs."

❑ Click on All Programs. All Programs will be highlighted. A sub-menu appears on the right.

❏   Glide the mouse across All Programs and up to the word Accessories.

❏   Click on Accessories. Glide the mouse across Accessories and down to Microsoft Interactive Training. A sub-menu appears on the right.

❏   Glide the mouse across Microsoft Interactive Training to the sub-menu.

❏   Click on Microsoft Interactive Training. The Select a Syllabus Window appears.

❏   Click on OK. The Microsoft Interactive Course Window appears on the left.

❏   Click on Microsoft Windows XP Home Edition. Using Microsoft Interactive Training appears on the list on the screen.

❏   Click on Using Microsoft Interactive Training. Introduction appears on the list on the screen.

❏   Click on Introduction. How to Use This Product appears on the list on the screen.

❏   Click on How to Use This Product. The training course begins in the right-hand screen. In the left-hand window, a red arrow appears next to the topic being explained in the right-hand window. The program moves forward automatically from topic to topic. You can exit or reenter at any point.

❏   Click on the red Exit Buttons in each window to exit. Desktop appears.

HELP AND SUPPORT CENTER

The Help and Support Center can be very confusing to the beginner. It is important to know it exists even though it will not be of much use until you become more familiar with your computer.   The easiest way to use the Help and Support Center is with the Index Button.

❏   Click on Start. The Start Menu appears on the screen.

❏   Click on Help and Support which appears in the right-hand column. The Help and Support Center window appears.

❏   Click on the Index Button which appears on the Navigation Bar at the top of the window. The Index scroll box appears on the left of the screen.

❏   Type in a keyword relating to the topic you are looking for in the text box above the scroll box. A list of subjects relating to the topic you selected appears in the scroll box.

❏   Click on the applicable subject to select it. The selection is highlighted.

❏   Click on the Display Button at the bottom of the scroll box. Information relating to the topic appears in the text box on the right.

IMPORTANT THINGS TO REMEMBER

When you place the cursor on underlined text which appears in the right-hand text box, the arrow on the cursor changes into a hand indicating it is a link to additional information. Click on the underlined text to access the additional information.

To print the text on the right-hand screen, click on the Print Button at the top of the right-hand screen.

Printing Help and Support Information

❑ Click on the Printer icon which appears above the right-hand text column. Only the information in the right-hand column will be printed.

❑ To exit from Help and Support, click on the Exit Button in the upper right-hand corner.

FILES AND FOLDERS - YOUR RECIPE BOX

In your kitchen you don't keep recipes lying around loose on every shelf or counter. You put them in a recipe box. You even separate them by soups, desserts, and salads. When you get a new recipe, you put it in the box under the proper category. When you want to use it, you know just where to find it.

Pretend that you just found a new recipe for apple pie. Where are you going to put it? Open your recipe box and look in the dessert section. Cakes are in a sub-section, pies are in another sub-section, and, in the pies' sub-section, there are sub-sections for fruit pies and cream pies.

Your computer organizes programs and files in the same way. Folders are the sections of your recipe box. Files are the recipes. Not only does a folder contain files, but it can also contain sub-folders. And sub-folders can also contain sub-folders! How many depends upon your needs.

In Windows everything is stored in folders. Some of the folders have been created by Windows to organize important elements that run your computer. Programs are found in other folders. You can create folders to organize and store your own documents.

Whenever you save a document that you have created, it must be named and stored as an individual file in a folder.

It is easy to tell a file from a folder because they have different symbols (called icons). In Windows, a folder is always a yellow icon which looks like a manila folder. A square icon indicates a file.

DESKTOP - THINK OF IT AS YOUR KITCHEN COUNTER

The screen that appears when you turn on your computer is called Desktop. On it are icons (shortcuts) that you click on with the mouse to give you direct access to specific programs and folders.

Which icons initially appear on Desktop vary with each computer. Every computer on which Windows is installed will probably contain an icon for "My Computer," a folder which enables you to view the contents of your computer and an icon for "Recycle Bin," a device to store files before their final deletion.

Don't be afraid to click on any of the icons which appear on Desktop. It is fun to look around. When you click on an icon a window appears. To exit, click on the Exit Button (the one with the X) which appears in the upper right-hand corner. You will be returned to Desktop.

As you become more skilled, you will add icons to Desktop for programs you have installed or folders you have created.

IT'S LIKE HAVING SEPARATE CLOSETS

Because Windows XP allows you to set up separate accounts for individual users, you can share your computer with others in your household and still maintain your privacy. Each account user automatically has separate files and settings and an exclusive Desktop screen. An individual account user cannot access another's files without permission. When the account user logs on to the computer, the name of the account user appears on the Welcome Screen and on the top of the Start Menu. A list of the account user's recently accessed programs appears in the left-hand column of the Start Menu. Passwords can also be attached to individual accounts.

Somebody Has To Be Boss!

Because only the Computer Administrator can create or delete a user account, in order to have multiple user accounts, one account must be selected to be the Computer Administrator. During the installation of your new computer, the owner is automatically designated as the Computer Administrator. It is possible to have another user become the Computer Administrator.

ESTABLISHING A COMPUTER ADMINISTRATOR

❑ Click on Start. The Start Menu appears.

❑ Click on Control Panel. The Control Panel Pick a Category window appears.

❑ Click on User Accounts. The User Account Pick a Task window appears.

❑ Click on Create a New Account. The Name the New Account dialog box appears.

❑ Enter the name of the person whom you want to be the Computer Administrator.

❑ Click on Next. The Pick an Account Type dialog box appears.

❑ Click on Computer Administrator. A description of the privileges associated with being the Computer Administrator is presented.

❑ Click on Create Account. The account is established.

CREATING A LIMITED USER ACCOUNT

❑ Click on Start. The Start Menu appears.

❑ Click on Control Panel. The Control Panel Pick a Category window appears.

❏ Click on User Accounts. The User Account Pick a Task window appears.

❏ Click on Create a New Account. The Name the New Account dialog box appears.

❏ Enter the name of the person to whom you want to assign an account.

❏ Click on Next. The Pick an Account Type dialog box appears.

❏ Click on Limited. A description of the privileges associated with a limited account is presented.

❏ Click on Create Account. The account is established.

ENTERING A PASSWORD

❏ Click on Start. The Start Menu appears.

❏ Click on Control Panel. The Control Panel Pick a Category window appears.

❏ Click on User Accounts. The User Account Pick a Task window appears.

❏ Click on the name of the account for which you want to establish a password. The What Do You Want to Change dialog box appears.

❏ Click on Create a Password. The Create a Password dialog box appears.

❏ Follow the instructions for entering the password.

❏ Click on Create Password. The What Do You Want to Change dialog box appears.

❏ Click on the Exit Button in the upper right-hand corner to exit.

SWITCHING FROM ONE USER ACCOUNT TO ANOTHER

❏ Click on Start. The Start Menu appears.

❏ Click on Log Off. The Log Off Window appears.

❏ Click on Switch User. The names of accounts appear on the screen.

❏ Click on the name of the account to which you want to switch. If the account has a password associated with it, enter the password and click on the arrow. The Welcome Screen appears. The Desktop screen associated with the account you are using appears.

❏ Click on the Start Menu. The Start Menu appears. The name of the current user account appears on top. The list of programs recently accessed by the current user account appears in the left-hand column.

DELETING A LIMITED ACCOUNT

In order to be able to delete an account, you must be logged on as the Computer Administrator.

❑ Click on Start. The Start Menu appears.

❑ Click on Control Panel. The Control Panel Pick a Category window appears.

❑ Click on User Accounts. The User Account Pick a Task window appears.

❑ Click on the name of the account which you wish to delete. The What Do You Want to Change dialog box appears.

❑ Click on Delete the Account. A dialog box appears asking if you want to keep the file associated with the account.

❑ Click on Keep Files or Delete Files. A window appears asking if you really want to delete the account.

❑ Click on Delete the Account. You are returned to the User Account Pick a Task Window.

❑ Click on the Exit Button in the upper right-hand corner to exit.

OPENING A PROGRAM –YOU HAVE TO START SOMEWHERE!

Turning on the computer is the same as opening a book. There are all those introductory pages that you have to flip through to get to Chapter One. With a book, you can skip everything and go right to where you want to begin reading. With a computer, you automatically view the opening pages and then must go through several steps to open the program you want to use.

❑ Turn on your computer. The screen identifying the installed version of Windows appears.

❑ Desktop appears. The Start Button appears on the Taskbar at the bottom of the screen.

TURNING ON THE COMPUTER IF SET UP FOR MULTIPLE USERS

❑ Turn on your computer. The screen identifying the installed version of Windows appears.

❑ The Welcome Screen appears.

❑ Click on the User Name. Desktop appears. The Start Button appears on the Taskbar at the bottom of the screen.

OPENING A PROGRAM USING THE PROGRAM COMMAND

❑ Click on Start. The Start Menu appears.

❑ Locate the "All Programs" command. It is usually above the Start Button. An arrowhead to its right indicates that sub-menus are attached to this command.

❑ Click on "All Programs." A sub-menu appears.

❑ If the name of the program you are looking for is visible in the sub-menu, glide the mouse across "All Programs" and up or down the sub-menu to the program you want to open. Click on it to open it.

If the name of the program is not yet visible, position the mouse arrow on names on the sub-menu list that have right arrowheads, gliding to open sub-menus for each one until the name of the program you want appears. Try "Accessories" first. Many of the programs that come with Windows are located in the "Accessories" sub-menus.

DON'T PANIC!

When you position the mouse on Programs, the sub-menu appears very quickly. Don't move the mouse until you know where you are going. Glide the mouse across Programs. Glide the mouse up or down the sub-menu to where you want to be. If you need to go to another sub-menu, glide over to it before you move the mouse up or down.

If you make a mistake, click on a blank spot on Desktop, which is still visible. The Start Menu will appear. Try again by clicking the Start Button.

If you open a program by mistake, close it by clicking on the Exit Button in the upper right-hand corner of the program window (The button with the X on it).

❑ Click on the program to open it.

OPENING A PROGRAM USING THE START MENU

❑ Click on Start. The Start Menu appears. The Start Menu consists of two columns located on the left of the screen above the Start Button.

The right-hand column has icons to important files. If you use a program frequently, an icon to it will appear in the left-hand column.

❑ If the icon for the program which you want to use appears in either column of the Start Menu, click on it to open it.

OPENING A PROGRAM USING A DESKTOP SHORTCUT ICON

❑ Turn on your computer. Desktop appears.

❑ If the icon to the program you want to open is on Desktop, double click on it to open it.

CLOSING A PROGRAM

❑ Click on the Exit Button. The Exit Button is located in the upper right-hand corner of every window. It is the button with an X on it.

SHUTTING DOWN YOUR COMPUTER - THERE'S MORE TO DO THAN TURNING OFF THE SWITCH

Windows XP offers several options for turning off the computer. You can close your files and turn the computer off completely. You can log off, a procedure in which the computer remains on, but access to your files remains closed until the computer is reactivated. Logging off is particularly useful if you have established multiple user accounts because another user can access the computer when you are finished without having to turn the computer on again.

TURNING OFF THE COMPUTER COMPLETELY

It is important to close all the programs before you turn off the computer. If you don't, you could damage any open files.

❑ Click on Start. The Start Menu appears on the screen.

❑ Click on Turn Off Computer. The Turn Off Computer dialog box appears on the screen.

❑ Click on Turn Off. The message "Windows is Shutting Down" appears on the screen.

❑ Do not turn off the computer until the screen is dark.

LOGGING OFF

❑ Click on Start. The Start Menu appears on the screen.

❑ Click on Log Off. The Log Off Windows dialog box appears on the screen.

❑ Click on Log Off. Your programs are closed. The computer remains on. The Welcome Screen appears.

❑ Click on the user name on the Welcome Screen to reactivate the computer.

INSTALLING A PROGRAM FROM A CD-ROM OR FLOPPY DISK

❑   Click on Start. The Start Menu appears.

❑   Click on Control Panel. The Control Panel dialog box appears.

❑   Click on Add or Remove Programs icon. The Add or Remove Programs dialog box appears.

❑   Click on Add New Programs which appears in the left-hand column.

❑   Click on the CD or Floppy Button. The Install Program from Floppy Disk or CD-ROM dialog box appears.

❑   Insert Floppy Disk or CD-ROM in the appropriate drive.

❑   Click on Next. The Run Installation Program dialog box appears. The name of the installation program should appear in the "Command line for installation program:" box.

❑   Click on Finish. The installation program is run. Follow any instructions that appear on the screen.

❑   In most cases an icon for the newly installed program will appear in the Start Menu.

LEARNING ABOUT WINDOWS

Chapter 2

THERE'S A BAR ON EVERY CORNER

Whenever you turn on your computer or open a program, long rectangular boxes or bars appear on the screen. It is important to understand the functions of these bars.

TASKBAR

The Taskbar appears on the screen as soon as you turn your computer on. It usually is at the bottom of the screen. The Start button is in the left-hand corner. The time appears in the right-hand corner.

When you open a program, the name of the program appears in a button on the Taskbar. If you have more than one program open, a name button appears for each program. When you close a program, the name button for that program disappears.

Using the Taskbar to Switch from One Program to Another

If you have several programs open at the same time, you can switch back and forth from one program to another by alternately clicking on the program name buttons on the Taskbar.

Moving the Taskbar

Although normally the Taskbar is located at the bottom of the screen, you can move it to either side or to the top. You must unlock the Taskbar before you can move it.

❑ Right click on any blank space on the Taskbar. A drop-down menu appears. There is a check next to Lock the Taskbar.

❑ Click on Lock the Taskbar. The check disappears. The drop-down menu disappears. The Taskbar is unlocked.

❑ Position the mouse arrow on a blank section of the Taskbar. Holding down the left mouse button, move the arrow to the new location. Release the mouse. The Taskbar appears in its new location.

❑ Right click on any blank space on the Taskbar to relock it. A drop-down menu appears.

❑ Click on Lock the Taskbar. The drop-down menu disappears. The Taskbar is locked.

Resizing the Taskbar

To make the Taskbar wider or narrower it is first necessary to unlock the Taskbar.

❑   Right click on any blank space on the Taskbar. A drop-down menu appears. There is a check next to Lock the Taskbar.

❑   Click on Lock the Taskbar. The drop-down menu disappears. The Taskbar is unlocked.

❑   Position the mouse arrow on the top border of the Taskbar. The arrow will turn into a double-headed arrow. Holding down the left mouse button, move the arrow to the desired width. An outline of the new width will appear on the screen. Release the mouse. The Taskbar's width has been changed.

❑   Right click on any blank space on the Taskbar to relock it. A drop-down menu appears.

❑   Click on Lock the Taskbar. The drop-down menu disappears. The Taskbar is locked.

TITLE BAR

When you open a window, the Title Bar appears at the top. The name of the window appears on the left. The Exit Button and the buttons to maximize or minimize the size of the window are on the right.

MENU BAR

The Menu Bar appears directly below the Title Bar. It consists of a row of commands specific to the program that you are running. When you click on any one of the command words, a drop-down menu appears listing options specific to that command.

Drop-Down Menus

- A command that appears in gray is not applicable at that moment.

- If a command has a check mark next to it, that option has been turned on. To turn off an option, click on the check mark to remove it. To turn on an option, click to its left to add a check mark.

- An arrowhead to the right of a command indicates that the command has a submenu of options. Click on the command to open the submenu.

- An ellipsis (...) to the right of a command indicates that further information is needed to activate the command. When you click on the command, a dialog box with blanks to be filled in will appear.

❑   Click on any blank space on the screen to close a drop-down menu. The drop-down menu will disappear.

TOOLBARS

A Toolbar consists of rows of icons and buttons that you click to carry out specific commonly used commands including opening files, printing, and text formatting. Toolbars are not displayed in all windows. If a Toolbar is present, it usually appears under the Menu Bar.

Identifying the Function of a Button or Icon on a Toolbar

Place the mouse arrow on top of the button or icon. Do not click on it. In a few seconds the function of the button or icon will appear on the screen in a small box. When you move the mouse, the box disappears.

Displaying Different Toolbars

There are many Toolbars. To choose the Toolbars you want to display:

❑   Click on View on the Menu Bar. A drop-down menu appears.

❑   Click on Toolbars. A sub-menu appears listing all the available Toolbars.

❑   Click on the left of the Toolbars you want to display.

❑   To close the drop-down menu, click on any blank space on the screen. The drop-down menu will disappear.

Removing a Toolbar from Display

❑   Click on View on the Menu Bar. A drop-down menu appears.

❑   Click on Toolbars. A sub-menu appears listing all the available Toolbars.

❑   Click on the checkmark to the left of the Toolbars you want to remove.

❑   To close the drop-down menu, click on any blank space on the screen. The drop-down menu will disappear.

SCROLL BARS

A Vertical Scroll Bar appears on the right side of the window. It consists of up and down arrow buttons and a scroll box. The position of the scroll box within the Vertical Scroll Bar corresponds to the position of the text that is visible on the screen to the rest of the file that is not displayed.

A Horizontal Scroll Bar appears at the bottom of the window. It consists of left and right arrow buttons and a scroll box. The position of the scroll box in the Horizontal Scroll box corresponds to the horizontal position of the text displayed in the file.

Scrolling allows you to move the screen horizontally or vertically to bring text that is not on the screen into view.

To Scroll Continuously

❑   Place the mouse on the appropriate arrow. Depress the left button. Keep the left button depressed until the desired text is visible.

To Scroll Vertically a Line at a Time or Horizontally a Character at a Time

❑   Click on the appropriate arrow.

To Move the Screen Approximately a Window at a Time

❑   Click the mouse in the scroll bar either above or below the scroll box.

To Move Quickly to a Specific Location

❑   Place the mouse on the scroll box and drag until the desired text is visible. This is particularly useful for a long file.

THE LEFT-HAND COLUMN

When you open certain files such as My Documents, My Computer, My Pictures, and Control Panel, the left-hand column of the window contains links to tasks which you may want to perform. These links are provided as shortcuts. They are more useful to experienced users than beginners. You can safely ignore the left-hand column until then.

Tasks are arranged by category including File and Folder Tasks, Other Places, and Details. Each category contains a circle with arrows.

❑   Click on the circle. The chosen category expands to display a list of options.

❑   Place the cursor on any option, but do not click. A description of the option appears on the screen.

❑   Click on any option to select it.

WINDOWS ARE NOT A PANE!

Think of windows as pieces of paper in a loose-leaf notebook. You can open the notebook, take out a few pages, stack one on top of another, view several pages at the same time, and move back and forth from one page to another.

Instead of spreading the pages out on a table, you rearrange them on the screen. You can resize them, move them, and even make them disappear. When you are finished, the Windows operating system puts the papers back in the notebook.

CLOSING A SINGLE WINDOW

❑ Click on the Exit Button in the upper right-hand corner of the Title Bar (the button with the X on it). The window will disappear.

CLOSING MULTIPLE WINDOWS

❑ Click on the Exit Button in the upper right-hand corner of the window that is in front of the screen. The window will disappear. Continue clicking on the Exit Button of each window.

MAXIMIZING THE SIZE OF A WINDOW

❑ Click on the Maximize Button on the Title Bar (the button with the square). The window will be enlarged to take up the whole screen. The Restore Button (two squares) replaces the Maximize Button on the Title Bar.

❑ To restore the window to its previous size, click the restore button.

MINIMIZING THE SIZE OF A WINDOW

❑ Click on the Minimize Button on the Title Bar (the button with the line on the bottom edge). The window disappears from the screen, but is still open.

❑ To display the window and restore it to its previous size, click on the name of the window which appears on the Taskbar.

WHERE DID THAT WINDOW GO?

When you have two or more windows open at the same time, the window which you opened last appears on top. Even though the other windows are not visible, they are still open.

The names of windows which are open, but not visible, appear on the Taskbar. To view any open window which is not visible, click on its name on the Taskbar.

By clicking on names on the Taskbar, you can alternate from one open window to another.

CHANGING THE SHAPE OF A WINDOW

You can make a window wider or taller. The shape that you create is only applicable to that particular window while it is currently open. When you close the window and reopen it, it will appear in its original shape.

❑ Position the mouse arrow on the top or bottom edge of the window. Pause a few seconds. The arrow will change into a double-headed arrow. Holding your finger down on the left mouse button, drag the window with the mouse. Release the mouse. The window will appear in its new shape.

❑ Position the mouse arrow on the left or right edge of the window. Pause a few seconds. The arrow will change into a double-headed arrow. Holding your finger down on the left mouse button, drag the window with the mouse. Release the mouse. The window will appear in its new shape.

❑ Position the mouse arrow on one of the corners of the window. Pause a few seconds. The arrow will change into a double-headed arrow. Holding your finger down on the left mouse button, drag the window with the mouse. Release the mouse. The window will appear in its new shape.

MOVING A WINDOW

❑ Position the mouse arrow on a blank space in the Title Bar. Holding down the left mouse button, move the arrow to the new location. Release the mouse. The window appears in its new location.

DISPLAYING MULTIPLE WINDOWS

When you open a window it normally takes up the whole screen. If you open other windows, they are layered on top of previously opened windows. This configuration allows you to see only one window at a time.   It is possible to view multiple windows at the same time.

Cascading Windows

❑ Open windows that you want to display simultaneously. Do not minimize the size of the windows.

❑ Right click on a blank space in the Taskbar. A drop-down menu appears.

❑ Click on Cascade. The windows appear in the cascading configuration, layering one window on top of another. The Title Bar of each window is visible. To display the screens of both windows at the same time, position the mouse arrow on a blank space in the Title Bar of the window which is on top. Hold down the left mouse button and move the arrow until the second window is visible.

To remove the cascade command:

❑ Right click on a blank space in the Taskbar. A drop-down menu appears.

❑ Click on Undo Cascade.   The windows return to their original configuration.

Tiling Vertically

Multiple windows can be displayed side-by-side in a vertical configuration.

❑ Open windows that you want to display simultaneously. Do not minimize the size of either of the windows.

❑ Right click on a blank space in the Taskbar. A drop-down menu appears.

❑ Click on Tile Vertically. A portion of each window appears vertically on the screen at one time.

To remove the vertical tiling:

❑ Right click on a blank space in the Taskbar. A drop-down menu appears.

❑ Click on Undo Tile. The windows return to the previous configuration.

Tiling Horizontally

Multiple windows can be displayed in a horizontal configuration.

❑ Open windows that you want to display simultaneously. Do not minimize the size of either of the windows.

❑ Right click on a blank space in the Taskbar. A drop-down menu appears.

❑   Click on Tile Horizontally. A portion of each window appears horizontally on the screen at one time.

To remove the horizontal tiling:

❑   Right click on a blank space in the Taskbar. A drop-down menu appears.

❑   Click on Undo Tile. The windows return to the previous configuration.

SWITCHING BACK AND FORTH FROM A WINDOW IN ONE PROGRAM TO A WINDOW IN ANOTHER PROGRAM

You can have more than one program open at a time. Each time a program is opened, the name of that program appears on a button on the Taskbar. The button remains on the Taskbar until the program is closed.

You can switch back and forth from one program to the other by alternately clicking on the program name buttons on the Taskbar.

MY DOCUMENTS –A SPECIAL CLOSET LETS YOU STORE EVERYTHING IN ONE PLACE

My Documents is a master folder which Windows automatically provides especially for you. My Documents helps you to organize your computer. It belongs to you. Unless you specify elsewhere, any file you create is automatically stored in My Documents. Although programs that make Windows run are not stored in My Documents, files generated by certain programs are automatically stored there.

My Documents always contains two sub-folders: My Pictures and My Music. If your grandchild sends you a picture you can save it in My Pictures. If you create a drawing in Paint you can also store it in My Pictures. You can store music in My Music. If you write a novel, it is stored in My Documents too. You can create as many folders and sub-folders as you want. If you create a file, you can also store it directly in My Documents without creating another sub-folder.

Using My Documents is an easy way to access your folders and files.

❑ Click on Start. The Start Menu appears. The icon for My Documents appears in the right-hand column of the Start Menu.

❑ Click on My Documents. The My Documents window appears. It contains two screens. In the right is list of all your personal files and folders. The left screen contains links to perform certain tasks, and to other places.

❑ Click on any folder or file to open it.

WINDOWS HAS MANY "RECIPES" FOR THE SAME TASK

Windows provides many ways to do the same thing. Often, which way you choose depends upon which window you are working in. My Documents offers links to performing tasks associated with files and folders. To perform a task using a link, click on the link and continue making the appropriate selections until the task is performed.

❑ Click on the Exit Button in the upper right-hand corner to exit.

MY COMPUTER - YOUR KITCHEN CABINET

My Computer is a master folder. In it you will find the contents of your computer. All your programs, folders, and files are accessible from My Computer. It is not essential for you to use My Computer but, if you are curious, open it up and look around.   If you familiarize yourself with My Computer, you will be comfortable using it to perform certain functions described later in this manual.

❑   Turn on your computer. Desktop appears on the screen.

❑   Click on Start. The Start Menu appears on the screen.

❑   Click on My Computer icon. The My Computer window appears. It contains two screens.

On the right-hand screen are icons for the hard disk [C:]; floppy disk [A:]; DVD/CD-RW drive [D:], if you have one; Internet server; and document files.

On the left-hand screen are options to perform System tasks, other places, and details. If you click on the encircled double arrows for each option, the screen expands to display choices.

IT'S YOUR CHOICE!

You can control the format in which the information appears on the right-hand screen.
❑   Click on Views on the Toolbar. It is the square white icon with small colored squares on it. A drop-down menu appears with the following viewing options:
Thumbnails – Icons in boxes arranged by categories with titles below.
Tiles – Icons are arranged by categories. Titles appear on the side.
Icon- Icons are arranged by categories with titles below.
List- Icons appear in a list with titles.
Detail- Icons are arranged by categories. Beside each are details including type, size, free space, and comments.
❑   Click on any option. A black dot appears indicating your choice.
❑   You can change options by clicking on Views on the Toolbar and making another selection.

❑   Click on any of the options on either screen.

❑   Click on the Exist Button in the upper right-hand corner of any window you open.

❑   Click on the Exit Button in the upper right-hand corner of My Computer to return to Desktop.

CONTROL PANEL – ANOTHER KITCHEN CABINET

Control Panel serves as a key to provide access to tools to use to adjust settings and customize Windows. Different tasks are arranged under broad categories. When you click on each category, a list of options appears. Select an option and the dialog box or menu associated with that option appears.

Many of the tasks which you access with Control Panel are explained in detail in other parts of this manual. For now, to discover all the things you can do to customize your computer, open Control Panel and look around.

❑ Click on Start. The Start Menu appears on the screen.

❑ Click on Control Panel which appears on the right-hand column of the Start Menu. The Control Panel window appears listing the following options:

- Appearance and Themes

- Network and Internet Connections

- Add or Remove Programs

- Sounds, Speech and Audio Devices

- Performance and Maintenance

- Printers and Other Hardware

- User Accounts

- Date, Time, Language, and Regional Options

- Accessibility Options

❑ Click on any one of the options. A list of tasks or Control Panel icons from which to choose appears.

❑ Click on any task or Control Panel icon. The Dialog box or menu associated with that task appears.

❑ Click on the Exit Button in the upper right-hand corner of any window you open

❑ Click on the Exit Button in the upper right-hand corner of Control Panel to return to Desktop.

WINDOWS EXPLORER – ONE MORE KITCHEN CABINET

Another way to see the contents of your computer is to open Windows Explorer. All your programs, folders, and files are accessible from Windows Explorer. Windows Explorer allows you to view a list of all folders and subfolders in one window and the contents of a particular folder or subfolder in another window simultaneously.

As you develop your computer skills, you will recognize the advantage of using Windows Explorer to perform many tasks. You will use it to copy, move, rename, or search for files and folders. There are several ways to open Windows Explorer, but the one described below is the easiest.

❑ Click on Start. The Start Menu appears on the screen.

❑ Click on All Programs. A sub-menu appears.

❑ Click on Accessories. A sub-menu appears.

❑ Click on Windows Explorer. A split screen appears. A list of all the drives and folders on your computer appears in the left window in a hierarchical or "tree" arrangement. A plus sign indicates that a folder or drive contains subfolders. Only folders, not individual files, appear in the left window. A list of the contents of whatever folder is highlighted appears in the right window.

TO DISPLAY A LIST OF SUBFOLDERS IN THE LEFT WINDOW

❑ Click on the plus sign to the left of a folder's name. The names and icons of the subfolders in that folder appear in the left window. The names of individual files contained in folders or subfolders are not displayed. The plus sign converts to a minus sign. The contents of the right window do not change.

TO REMOVE THE DISPLAYED LIST OF SUBFOLDERS IN THE LEFT WINDOW

❑ Click on the minus sign to remove the names of the subfolders in the left window. The plus sign reappears. The right window does not change.

TO DISPLAY THE CONTENTS OF A FOLDER OR SUBFOLDER IN THE RIGHT WINDOW

❑ Click on a folder's icon in the left window. The name of the folder is highlighted. The folder's icon changes from a closed folder to an open folder.

IT'S YOUR CHOICE!

You can control the format in which the information appears on the right-hand screen.

❑ Click on Views on the Toolbar. It is the square white icon with small colored squares on it. A drop-down menu appears with the following viewing options:

Thumbnails – Icons in boxes are arranged by categories with titles below.
Tiles – Icons are arranged by categories. Titles appear on the side.
Icon- Icons are arranged by categories with titles below.
List- Icons appear in a list with titles.
Detail- Icons appear in a list which includes size, type, and date modified.

❑ Click on any option. A black dot appears indicating your choice.

❑ You can change options by clicking on Views on the Toolbar and making another selection.

TO OPEN A FILE IN THE RIGHT WINDOW

❑ Click on the icon of any file or folder in the right window to open it. Files cannot be opened in the left window.

❑ To exit, click on the Exit Button in the upper right-hand corner.

WORKING WITH FILES
AND FOLDERS

Chapter 3

CREATING A FILE USING MICROSOFT WORD

Word is a text-processing program. It is a typewriter with a brain. Windows XP comes with two other text-processing programs. Wordpad is a less sophisticated program than Word. It is similar in format to Word, but does not include as many formatting and editing options. Notepad is an unsophisticated program used for brief text documents that require no formatting.

The instructions which follow are for Word. If you don't have Word, the instructions can easily be applied for use with Wordpad.

❑   Click on Start on the Taskbar. The Start Menu appears.

❑   Position mouse on All Programs. A sub-menu appears.

❑   Position mouse on Microsoft Word. A blank screen appears.

DON'T GIVE UP!

Everybody goofs here - it may take several tries to get it right. When you position the mouse on All Programs, the sub-menu appears very quickly. If you move the mouse before you know where you are going, sub-menus will appear from all directions.

Click on a blank spot on Desktop, which is still visible. The Start Menu and all the sub-menus will disappear. You can now try again by clicking the Start Button.

Do not move the mouse from All Programs until you locate Microsoft Word on the next menu. To move to Microsoft Word, glide the mouse across All Programs to the column containing Microsoft Word and up to Microsoft Word.

❑   Click on Microsoft Word.   The Microsoft Word window appears. It contains the following:

   •   Title Bar - "Microsoft Word" appears on left. On the right are the buttons to minimize or maximize the window and the Exit Button.

   •   Menu Bar - A row of commands. When you click on any of the command words, a drop- down menu appears listing options specific to the command.

   •   Toolbar – A row of icons and buttons that you click to carry out specific commands. To identify the function of an icon or button, place the mouse arrow on the icon or button. Do not click on it. In a few seconds the function of the button or icon will appear on the screen in a small box. When you move the mouse, the box disappears.

- Scroll Bar - A vertical bar on the right of the window that enables you to view the contents of the window by scrolling.

- Blank screen - The part of the window where you enter text.

ENTERING TEXT

Type the text in exactly the same way as you would if you were using a typewriter. The cursor is always visible, indicating the current insertion point. You can always change the insertion point to wherever you wish on the screen by moving the cursor to the place where you want to insert text and clicking on the mouse.

Word automatically moves to the next line as you enter text. If you want to create a new line or paragraph, press the Enter Key on the keyboard.

WANT TO CORRECT YOUR MISTAKES?

Right now it is important to learn how to save your document as a file and to create a folder in which to put it. Instructions for making corrections and additions to your newly created text are found in the section on Editing Your Documents.

SAVING A NEWLY CREATED FILE

In order to save a newly created file you must assign a name to it. You must also place it in a folder. The master folder for text files is called "My Documents."

ANOTHER "MY DOCUMENT" FOLDER

Microsoft Word stores all the documents you create using Word in a folder called "My Documents." This is not the same "My Document" folder which appears on the Start Menu. The Microsoft Word "My Document" folder contains only the files and folders which you create plus any other files and folders which you decide to store there.

The "My Document" folder which appears on the Start Menu contains all the files and folders that you have stored in the Microsoft Word "My Document" folder in addition to any files and folders generated automatically by other programs.

A newly created file can be placed directly in the "My Documents" folder. A newly created file can also be placed in an existing sub-folder in "My Documents." If the sub-folder in which you want to place it does not exist, you must create a new folder.

NAMING A NEWLY CREATED FILE AND SAVING IT IN "MY DOCUMENTS"

❑ Click on File on the Menu Bar. A drop-down menu appears.

❑ Click on Save As. The Save As dialog box appears.

❑ In the "File name:" box, the highlighted first few words of your document appear.

❑ Press the Backspace Key on the keyboard. The highlighted words disappear.

❑ Type the name you are assigning to the document in the "File name:" box.

A file or folder can have up to 255 characters in its name. It cannot include any of the following characters: | * \ < >? / ":

❑ "My Documents" appears in the "Look-in:" box.

❑ Click on Save. You are returned to the Word document. The title you assigned to the file appears in the left-hand corner of the Title Bar.

❑ Click on the small X in the right-hand corner of the Menu Bar to close the document.

❑ Click on the Exit Button in the upper right-hand corner to exit from Word.

NAMING A NEWLY CREATED FILE AND SAVING IT IN AN EXISTING SUB-FOLDER

❑ Click on File on the Menu Bar. A drop-down menu appears.

❑ Click on Save As. The Save As dialog box appears.

❑ In the "File name:" box, the highlighted first few words of your document appear.

❑ Press the Backspace Key on the keyboard. The highlighted words disappear.

❑ Type the name you are assigning to the document in the "File name:" box.

A file or folder can have up to 255 characters in its name. It cannot include any of the following characters: | * \ < >? / ":

❑ "My Documents" appears in the "Look-in:" box. A list of all the files and folders in "My Documents" appears on the screen.

❑ Double click on the folder in which you want to place the newly created file. The name of the folder appears in the "Look-in:" box. A list of all the files in the folder appears on the screen.

❑ Click on Save. You are returned to the Word document. The title you assigned to the file appears in the left-hand corner of the Title Bar.

❑ Click on the small X in the right-hand corner of the Menu Bar to close the document.

❑ Click on the Exit Button in the upper right-hand corner to exit from Word.

CREATING AND NAMING A NEW FOLDER AND SAVING A NEWLY CREATED FILE IN IT

❑ Click on File on the Menu Bar. A drop-down menu appears.

❑ Click on Save As. The Save As dialog box appears.

❑ In the "File name:" box, the highlighted first few words of your document appear.

❑ Press the Backspace Key on the keyboard. The highlighted words disappear.

❑ Type the name you are assigning to the document in the "File name:" box.

A file or folder can have up to 255 characters in its name. It cannot include any of the following characters: | * \ < >? / ":

❑ "My Documents" appears in the "Look-in:" box.

❑ Click on Create New Folder Button (the yellow file folder with a star behind it that appears on the same line as the "Look in:" box). The New Folder dialog box appears on the screen.

❑ Type the name you are assigning to the folder in the Name box.

❑ Click OK. The Save As dialog box appears. The name of the new folder appears in the "Look in:" box. The name of the new folder appears in the "File name:" box.

❑ Do not change what appears in the "Save as type:" box.

❑ Click on Save. You are returned to the Word document. The title you assigned to the file appears in the left-hand corner of the Title Bar.

❑ Click on the small X in the right-hand corner of the Menu Bar to close the document.

❑ Click on the Exit Button in the upper right-hand corner to exit from Word.

SAVING CHANGES TO A FILE THAT HAS ALREADY BEEN NAMED AND SAVED

After you have saved a file, you do not have to exit. You can continue adding and editing text. To save your additions, click on the Save Button that appears on the Toolbar. (It looks like a television screen). There is no written notification that the file has been saved.

It is a good idea to click on the Save Button frequently when you are working in a document.

Before exiting, click on the Save Button. If you forget to click it, a reminder appears on the screen asking you if you want to save any changes.

Anytime you reopen a file and make additional changes, save your changes by clicking on the Save Button.

EDITING YOUR DOCUMENTS

Using a computer to edit what you've written is wonderful! An eraser is a thing of the past. Mistakes can be corrected immediately or later. Additional text can be inserted at any time.

You can print your document at any stage, save it on your computer to print or refer to later, or even attach it to an e-mail. Many of the editing techniques you learn here will help you to write e-mails.

SAVING YOUR FILES

A very good habit to get into is to save your files every few minutes by clicking on the Save Button on the Toolbar.

Except for the first time you save a file, when you click on the Save Button you receive no notification that the file has been saved.

USING THE MOUSE TO SELECT TEXT FOR DELETION, MOVING, OR COPYING

Word allows you to delete, move, or copy single words or multiple lines of text at one time. Before text can be deleted, moved or copied, it must be selected using the mouse. Text that has been selected appears on the screen surrounded by a black highlighting.

It takes a few tries to master some of the selection techniques. It is well worth a few minutes to learn how.

GET INTO TROUBLE?

Even an expert will make a mistake and select the wrong text. Cancel your mistake by clicking once on any blank space in the screen. The black highlighting disappears. You are ready to begin again.

You can also cancel a mistake by clicking on the Undo Button on the Toolbar (the one that looks like an arrow with a tail). It will cancel the last thing you did.

If you get really mixed up, you can always exit the file without saving the changes. Click on the Exit Button. A message appears asking if you want to save the changes. Click "No." The file will be closed. All the corrections (or mistakes) since the last time you saved the file will disappear. Reopen the file and start again.

To Select a Single Word

❏ Double click anywhere on the word.

To Select an Entire Paragraph

❏ Triple click anywhere in the paragraph.

To Select a Single Line or Text

❏ Insert cursor and, holding the mouse button down, drag mouse over the text to be selected. Release the mouse button

To Select Multiple Lines of Text

❏ Insert cursor and, holding the mouse button down, drag the mouse over the first line and then either up or down to the next lines to be selected. Release the mouse button.

To Select an Entire Document:

❏ Click on Edit on the Menu Bar. A drop-down menu appears.

❏ Click on Select All. The entire text is highlighted.

DELETING USING THE BACKSPACE KEY OR THE DELETE KEY

Deleting Individual Words, Sentences, or Multiple Lines of Type

❏ Select the text to be deleted. Press the Backspace Key or the Delete Key. The selected text will be deleted.

Deleting Characters One at a Time

The Backspace Key erases the characters, blank spaces, and blank lines to the left of the blinking cursor one at a time. It is not necessary to select the characters to be deleted.

The Delete Key erases the characters, blank spaces and blank lines to the right of the blinking cursor one at a time. It is not necessary to select characters to delete them.

INSERTING TEXT

To insert text in an existing sentence, position the cursor "I" to the left of the character or space where you want to insert new text. Click on the mouse to activate the blinking cursor. Begin typing. The new text will appear to the left of the blinking cursor.

DELETING AND INSERTING TEXT AT THE SAME TIME

Select the text to be deleted. Begin typing. The highlighted text will disappear as soon as you type the first new character.

MOVING TEXT BY DRAGGING WITH THE MOUSE

Select the text to be moved. Position the mouse arrow anywhere on the selected text. Depress the left mouse button. Do not release it. A box appears attached to the arrow. Position the arrow at the place where you want to move the text. A dotted-line cursor appears. Release the mouse button. The text appears in its new location.

STRANGE THINGS APPEAR!

If you are using Microsoft Word 2002, the paste symbol appears next to the text which you have moved by dragging. It also appears when you cut and paste. It is a symbol used for more advanced editing. Pay no attention to it. As soon as you type additional text or close the file, it will disappear.

CUTTING AND PASTING

Cutting and Pasting is a technique to move text from one part of a document to another. You can also use it to move text from one document to another.

❑   Select the text that you want to move.

❑   Click on the Cut Button (the one that looks like a scissors). The highlighted text will disappear from the screen.

❑   Insert the cursor where you want to paste the text that you cut. To move the text to another document, open the other document and insert the cursor where you want to paste the text.

❑   Click on the Paste Button (the one that looks like a clipboard). The text will reappear in its new location.

COPYING TEXT

Text can be copied so that it appears in more than one location in a document. It can also be copied so that it appears in more than one document.

❑   Select the text that you want to copy.

❑   Click on the Cut Button (the one that looks like a scissors). The highlighted text disappears.

❑ Insert the cursor at the place where the text originally was.

❑ Click on the Paste Button (the one that looks like a clipboard). The text reappears in its old location.

❑ Insert the cursor where you want to paste the text that you cut. To move the text to another document, open the other document and insert the cursor where you want to past the text.

❑ Click on the Paste Button. The text now appears in both its new and old locations. If you want the text to appear in more than one other location, continue inserting the cursor in the chosen locations, clicking the Paste Button each time.

UNDO AND REDO BUTTONS

The Undo Button and the Redo Button each have an arrow with a tail on it. They enable you to correct a mistake immediately without editing. If you want to delete something you have just typed, click on the Undo Button. It will remove it. If you change your mind, click on the Redo Button. It will replace it.

FIND BUTTON

The Find Button is used to locate particular words or phrases throughout the entire text. It is a good way to check for consistency.

❑ Click on Edit on the Menu Bar. A drop-down window appears.

❑ Click on Find. The Find dialog box appears.

❑ Type In the "Find what:" box the word or phrase you want to locate.

To indicate that you want to match the whole word only or match the case click on the More Button. A detailed dialog box appears. Indicate your choices by clicking on the appropriate boxes.

❑ Click on the Find Next Button. The word you seek will be highlighted. You can edit it immediately by clicking on it and entering changes.

❑ Continue clicking on the Find Next Button until a message stating that the entire document has been searched appears.

❑ Click on OK.

❑ Click on the Exit Button in the Find dialog box to exit.

REPLACE BUTTON

The Replace Button is used to replace particular words or phrases throughout the entire text. You may choose whether to replace particular words or phrases all at once or one at a time each instance they occur.

❑   Click on Edit on the Menu Bar. A drop-down window appears.

❑   Click on Replace. The Find and Replace dialog box appears.

❑   In the "Find what:" box type in the word or phrase you want to locate.

   If you want to indicate whether you want to match the   whole word only or match the case click on the More Button. A detailed dialog box appears. Indicate your choices by clicking on the appropriate boxes.

❑   In the "Replace with:" box type the word or phrase with which you want to replace the word or phrase.

Replacing Words or Phrases One at a Time

❑   Click on the Find Next Button. The word or phrase that you want to replace is highlighted.

❑   Click on the Replace Button. The word or phrase is replaced.

❑   Continue clicking on the Replace Button until notification appears on the screen that all the replacements have been made.

❑   Click on OK.

❑   Click on the Exit Button in the Replace dialog box to exit.

Replacing All the Designated Words or Phrases at One Time

❑   Click on the Replace All Button. The replacements are made. Notification is given of the number of replacements made.

❑   Click on OK.

❑   Click on the Exit Button in the Replace dialog box to exit.

FORMATTING YOUR DOCUMENTS

Your computer is usually set for standard paper size and margins. This is called the "default" setting. The settings for any document file can be changed to create any size or form of document you want. Your file can be designed to be printed as a letter, an index card, an article, or an envelope. You can set margins, indentations, and alignments. Type styles sizes and colors can be changed.

IT IS IMPORTANT TO REMEMBER

- The file in which you want to make formatting changes must be open.
- The formatting changes you make apply only to that open file on which you are working unless you change the default settings.
- When you save the file, the formatting changes are saved too.
- Whenever you open that file, the formatting changes will apply.

PAGE LAYOUT SETTINGS

❑ Click on File on the Menu Bar of the file you want to format. A drop-down menu appears.

GET INTO TROUBLE?

If you make a mistake and a drop-down menu appears on the screen that you want to remove, click on any spot on the screen. The drop-down menu disappears.

If you want to remove a dialog box without making any changes, click cancel. The dialog box disappears.

If you have not yet clicked OK, you can cancel changes you have entered in a dialog box by clicking cancel. The dialog box will disappear.

❑ Click on Page Setup. The Page Setup dialog box appears.

Setting Paper Size

❑ Click on the Paper tab. The Paper Size window appears.

❑ Scroll in the "Paper Size:" box to find the correct paper size. Click on your choice to highlight it. Your selection will appear in the "Paper Size:" box.

Setting Margins and Paper Orientation

❑ Click on the Margins tab. The Margins window appears.

❑ Click on the Scroll Buttons in each of the boxes to select margin sizes.

❑ Click on the box next to Portrait or Landscape to set the paper orientation.

Saving Page Setup Changes

❑ Click on OK. The document for which you are activating Page Setup appears.

TABS

❑ Click on View on the Menu Bar. A drop-down menu appears.

MISSING A COMMAND IN THE DROP-DOWN MENU?

Frequently when you click on a command on the Menu Bar to access the drop-down menu, all the options offered by the drop-down menu do not appear on the screen. This is a space saving device. Double down-arrows at the bottom of the drop-down menu indicate that there are other options. Click on the arrows to view the entire drop-down menu.

❑ Click on Ruler. The Ruler Toolbar appears at the top of the screen.

❑ Click on the Ruler Toolbar wherever you want to insert a tab. A black mark indicates where you have positioned a tab. You can insert as many tabs as you want.

❑ To remove a tab, place the mouse on the black mark. A vertical broken line appears. Drag the black mark either to the left or right until it is out of the window.

PARAGRAPH SETTINGS

Setting Alignment and Indents for Paragraphs and Line Spacing Using the Paragraph Dialog Box

❑ Click on Format on the Menu Bar. A drop-down menu appears.

❑ Click on Paragraph. The Paragraph dialog box appears.

❑ Click on the Indents and Spacing tab. Boxes in which to type in settings for alignment, margins, indents and line spacing appear.

❏ Scroll on the appropriate boxes to enter the appropriate settings. Each time you make a selection, an image of how the text will appear is shown on the Preview screen at the bottom of the window.

❏ Click on OK. The Word window appears.

Setting Indents for Paragraphs Using the Ruler

❏ Click on View on the Menu Bar. A drop-down menu appears.

❏ Click on Ruler. The Ruler Toolbar appears at the top of the screen.

❏ Drag the arrow on the top of the ruler that is pointing downward to set size of the indent of the first line of the paragraph.

❏ Drag the left or right arrow on the bottom of the ruler that point upward to set the distance from the left or right margin that you want to place the paragraph.

FORMATTING BAR

The Formatting Bar is the most useful for performing common editing functions which include changing font type and size, inserting bold, underlined or italicized characters, aligning text and changing text colors, among others.

❏ Click on View on the Menu Bar. A drop-down menu appears.

❏ Click on Toolbars. A drop-down menu appears.

❏ Click on Formatting. The Formatting Bar appears on the screen below the Toolbar. It consists of rows of buttons, which are used to carry out specific commands.

To identify the function of a button on the Format Bar, place the mouse arrow on top of the button. In a few seconds the button's function will appear in a small box.

Changing Fonts (Type Styles)

The name of the font in the Font Box is that of the font that is currently in use.

Changing Fonts Before Entering Text in a New Document

❏ Click on the arrow in the Font Box. A drop-down list appears containing the names of available fonts.

❏ Click on a font to select it. The drop-down list disappears. The name of the newly selected font appears in the Font Box. The text you enter will be in the new font.

Changing Fonts for Text Already Entered

Select the text that you want to appear in a different font.

❑ The name of the font in the Font Box is that of the font that is currently in use.

❑ Click on the arrow in the Font Box. A drop-down list appears containing the names of the available fonts.

❑ Click on a font to select it. The drop-down list disappears. The name of the newly selected font appears in the Font Box. The highlighted text appears in the new font.

❑ Click on the highlighted text to remove the highlighting. The name of the original font appears in the Font Box.

Inserting Additional Text in a New Font

❑ Insert the cursor at the point where you want the new font to appear.

❑ The name of the font in the Font Box is that of the font that is currently in use.

❑ Click on the arrow in the Font Box that is on the left of the screen. A drop-down list appears containing the names of the available fonts.

❑ Click on a font to select it. The drop-down list disappears. The name of the new font appears in the Font Box. The new font appears as you type. If you move the cursor to another insertion point, the original font will return.

Changing Font Sizes

The Font Size Box appears in the middle of the Format Bar.

To change font sizes follow the instructions for changing fonts, substituting the Font Size Box for the Font Box.

Creating Bold, Italicized, Or Underlined Text

To Make the Text of an Entire Document Bold, Italicized or Underlined

❑ Click on the Bold, Italics, or Underline button. The text will appear in the chosen style. It is possible to have bold, italicized, and underlined text all at one time.

To Include Bold, Italicized or Underlined Text While You Are Typing

❑ Click on the Bold, Italics, or Underline button.

❑ Insert the cursor at the point where you want the bold, italicized or underlined text to begin.

❑ As you continue typing, the text you enter will be in the chosen format.

❑ Click on the Bold Italicize or Underline button to return to normal text.

To Change Text Which Has Already Been Entered Into Bold, Italicized or Underlined Text

❑ Select the text that you want to make bold, italicized or underlined.

❑ Click on the Bold, Italics, or underline button.

❑ The highlighted text will appear in the style you have chosen.

❑ Click on the highlighted text to remove the highlighting.

Aligning Text

The text of a document can be aligned against the left margin, against the right margin, or centered.

Aligning a Document Before Entering Text

❑ Click on the appropriate button. The entire document will be aligned according to your selection.

Aligning a Document After the Text Has Been Entered

❑ Click on Edit on the Menu Bar. A drop-down menu appears.

❑ Click on Select All. The entire text is highlighted.

❑ Click on the appropriate button. The entire document will be aligned according to your selection.

Aligning Part of the Text

❏ Select the part of the text that you want to align by clicking on the mouse and gliding the mouse over the text to highlight it.

❏ Click on the appropriate button. The text you selected is realigned.

❏ Click on the realigned text to remove the highlighting box.

❏ Click on the appropriate button to return to the previous alignment or to go to another alignment

Changing Text Color

Changing Colors Before Entering Text

❏ Click on the Color Button. A color chart appears.

❏ Click on a color to select it. The color chart disappears. The entire document will appear in the color of choice.

Changing Colors of the Entire Text After the Text Has Been Entered

❏ Click on Edit on the Menu Bar. A drop-down menu appears.

❏ Click on Select All. The entire text is highlighted.

❏ Click on the Color Button. A color chart appears.

❏ Click on a color to select it. The color chart disappears.

❏ Click on any blank spot on the screen. The entire document appears in the color of choice.

Changing Colors for Part of the Text

❏ Select the part of the text that you want to change color.

❏ Click on the Color Button. A color chart appears.

❏ Click on a color to select it. The color chart disappears.

❏ Click on the highlighted text to remove the highlighting box.

❏ The selected text appears in the color of choice.

❏ Click on the Color Button and click on the previous color to return to it.

PRINTING YOUR FILES - WHY NOT COPY YOUR RECIPES!

The easiest thing to do with a computer is print. There are two ways to print a file. One way is to push a button and print one copy just the way you entered it. The other way offers options such as printing multiple copies or printing only selected pages. You can also preview on the screen just how your file will look on the printed page. You are limited by the capabilities of your printer.

PREVIEWING YOUR FILE

❑ Click on the Print Preview icon on the Toolbar (the white icon with the magnifying glass in the right-hand corner). The page of the file in which you are working appears on the screen as it will appear on the printed page. You cannot make any corrections to the file in Print Preview.

To view other pages in the file, use the Scroll Bar on the right-hand side of the screen.

❑ Click on the red Exit Button in the upper right-hand corner. The file in which you were working appears on the screen.

PRINTING USING THE PRINTER ICON ON THE TOOLBAR

❑ Open the file that you want to print.

❑ Click on the Printer Icon on the Toolbar (the one that looks like a photocopier with paper).

❑ The entire file is printed.

PRINTING USING THE FILE COMMAND ON THE MENU BAR

❑ Open the file that you want to print.

❑ Click on File on the Menu Bar. A drop-down menu appears.

❑ Click on Print. The Print dialog box appears. It offers the following options:

 • Print range - click on the appropriate circle. To print particular pages, enter the pages to be printed in the box next to pages, following the instructions which appear below the box.

 • Copies - enter the desired number of copies by clicking on the scroll box.

- Collate – if the Collate Button is checked, the pages will be printed from the last page forward. If the Collate Button is not checked, the pages will be printed from the first page forward.

- Properties - the Properties option is in the upper right-hand corner of the dialog box. Another dialog box appears associated with your particular printer. It provides other printer options.

❑ Click on OK. The document is printed.

YOU REALLY CAN DO TWO THINGS AT THE SAME TIME!

When you send a file to the printer, your computer automatically makes a special copy of the file for the printer to use. The printer prints this copy of the file, not the actual file. Because the printer is printing the copy, you can continue to work in the actual file while the copy is being printed. The changes that you make to the file while the computer is printing will not appear in the copy that is currently being printed. You can even close the file that is printing and open another file to work on.

PRINTING THE CURRENT SCREEN

Occasionally it can be useful to print the contents of the screen that is currently displayed on your monitor.

❑ On the keyboard depress the Alt key and the Print Screen key. There will be no indication on the screen that anything happened.

❑ Position the cursor where you want to insert the printed copy of the screen. It can be inserted in the current file or in another file.

❑ Click on Paste on the Toolbar. A copy of the screen will appear where you placed it.

❑ To print, click on the print icon on the Toolbar.

REOPENING A FILE

There are several ways to reopen a file. You can click on the Word icon which appears on the Start Menu or on the Word icon located on Desktop. You can also click on the My Documents icon on the Start Menu.

If you reopen a file using the My Documents icon on the Start Menu, links to other tasks appear in the left-hand column. If you reopen a file using the Word icon, different links appear. Until you are ready to use the links, it really doesn't matter which way you do it. Clicking on the Word icon is quicker.

REOPENING A FILE USING MY DOCUMENTS ICON ON THE START MENU

❑   Click on Start. The Start Menu appears.

❑   Click on My Documents. The My Documents window appears. It contains a list of folders and files in the right-hand screen.

HOW DO YOU TELL A FILE FROM A FOLDER?

The name of a folder always has the symbol of a yellow folder on its left. The name of a Word document file always has a square symbol with the letter W superimposed on it.

DON'T FORGET! MY DOCUMENTS IS A FOLDER

When you open My Documents, the alphabetical list of folders may be followed by a list of Word document files. These Word documents files are files you created, but did not place in special folders. When a file is created and not placed in a special folder, it automatically is placed in the folder "My Documents" and appears in the window under its own name.

❑   If the name of the file appears on the screen, double click on the file name to open it.

❑   If the name of the file that you want to open is in a sub-folder, click on the appropriate folder until its name appears.

❑   Double click on the file to open it.

REOPENING A FILE USING MICROSOFT WORD ICON ON THE START MENU

❑   Click on Start. The Start Menu appears.

❑   Position mouse on Programs. A sub-menu appears.

❑ Locate Microsoft Word on the sub-menu. Glide the mouse across Programs and down to Microsoft Word.

❑ Click on Microsoft Word. The Microsoft Word window appears with a blank screen.

❑ Click on the Open File icon on the Toolbar. (The Open File icon is an open yellow file folder). A list of files and folders in the Windows folder appears in the right-hand screen. If the file is not in a sub-folder, it will appear under its own name.

If the name of the file that you want to open is in a sub-folder, click on the appropriate folder until the file name appears.

FOLDERS COME BEFORE FILES!

Whenever a list of folders and files appears on the screen, all the folders, arranged alphabetically, appear first. Files which are not in sub-folders appear alphabetically after the folders.

❑ Double click on the file to open it.

LOCATING FILES AND FOLDERS - I KNOW I PUT THAT RECIPE SOMEWHERE!

Last week you created a file. You did all the right things - you edited it, saved it, and turned off the computer. You are sure it is in the computer somewhere. But where!

USING THE SEARCH COMMAND

- ❑ Click on Start. The Start Menu appears.

- ❑ Click on Search. The Search Results window appears.

- ❑ Click on All Files or Folders which appears on the list in the left-hand panel of the window. The Search by any or all of the criteria below dialog box appears in the left-hand panel.

- ❑ Type in the name or part of the name of the file you are looking for in the "All or part of the file name:" box.

- ❑ If you do not remember the name, enter a word or phrase that appears in the file in the "A word or a phrase in the file:" box. It is not necessary to enter information in both the file name and phrase boxes.

- ❑ Click on the Search Button. The progress of the search appears in the left-hand panel.

  Whenever a file is found that contains the words you have entered in the "All or part of the file name:" box or in the "A word or a phrase in the file:" box, the name of all appropriate files will appear in the window on the right. Included are the name, folder, size, type, and date modified.

  If the file you are looking for appears on the screen before the search is completed, you can stop the search by clicking on the Stop Button.

- ❑ Double click on the file to open it. The Search Results window is automatically closed.

Can't Remember the Name or a Phrase?

Open Windows Explorers and click on the folders in the left window until the file or folder you are looking for appears in the right window.

FINDING OUT ABOUT YOUR FILES

Word keeps detailed records about Word files that you have created and stored on your computer. It is very easy to access these records.

❑ Open any file that you want to track.

❑ Click on File on the Menu Bar. A drop-down menu appears.

❑ Click on Properties. The Properties window appears. It contains five tabs: General, Summary, Statistics, Contents, and Custom. The tab that will probably be of most interest to you is Statistics.

❑ Click on the Statistics Tab. A window appears detailing the dates the file was created, modified, accessed, and printed. It includes data on the number of pages, paragraphs, lines, words and characters, as well as the number of revisions and time spent.

COPYING FILES OR FOLDERS

These instructions do not apply to copying files to floppy disks. (See instructions for copying using floppy disks and CDs).

COPYING FILES OR FOLDERS FROM ONE FOLDER TO ANOTHER

If you copy one folder to another folder, the folder that you copied becomes a subfolder. All the files that are in the folder that you copied to the new folder are automatically copied with the folder.

❑ Right click on the name or icon of the file or folder that you want to copy. A drop-down menu appears.

❑ Click on Copy.

❑ Locate the folder where you want to copy the file or folder.

❑ Right click on the name or icon of the folder. A drop-down menu appears.

❑ Click on Paste. The file or folder is now in both its new location and its old location.

COPYING FILES OR SUB-FOLDERS WITHIN THE SAME FOLDER

❑ Right click on the name or icon of the file or folder that you want to copy. A drop-down menu appears.

❑ Click on Copy.

❑ Right click on a blank space on the screen. A drop-down menu appears.

❑ Click on Paste. A copy of the file or folder appears on the screen labeled "Copy of " file or folder name.

MOVING FILES OR FOLDERS

Files can be moved from one folder to another. If you move one folder to another folder, the folder that you move becomes a subfolder. When you move a folder, all the files that are in that folder remain in the folder and are automatically moved with it.

❑ Right click on the name or icon of the file or folder that you want to move. A drop-down menu appears.

❑ Click on Cut.

❑ Locate the folder where you want to move the file or folder.

❑ Right click on the name or icon of the file or folder or on a blank space in the window. A drop-down menu appears.

❑ Click on Paste. The file or folder is now in its new location.

DELETING A FILE OR FOLDER

If you delete a folder, all the subfolders and files stored in that folder are automatically deleted. When you delete a file or folder, it automatically is sent to the Recycle Bin. This is a safety feature. The deleted file remains in the Recycle Bin and can be reinstated at any time. It is permanently deleted only when you empty the Recycle Bin. (See Recycle Bin).

❑ Right click on the name or icon of the folder or file that you want to delete. A drop-down menu appears.

❑ Click on Delete. The Confirm File Delete box appears. It asks if you really want to delete the file or folder and send it to the Recycle Bin.

❑ Click on Yes. If you decide you do not want to make the delete, click on No.

❑ To exit click on the Exit Button in the upper right-hand corner.

RENAMING A FILE OR FOLDER

❑ Right click on the name or icon of the file or folder that you want to rename. A drop-down menu appears.

❑ Click on Rename. The old name of the file or folder is now enclosed in a box.

❑ Type in the new name. The old name will disappear.

❑ Click on a blank space on the screen. The name is now changed. The file or folder will be alphabetized on the screen under its new name.

❑ To exit click on the Exit Button in the upper right-hand corner.

CREATING A NEW FOLDER - IT'S LIKE REARRANGING YOUR RECIPE BOX

The time will come when you will want to rearrange some of your files and folders. You will probably need a new folder in which to put them. Although you are able to create a folder at the same time that you create a file, the instructions below are for creating empty folders in which files can be placed later. New folders can be created when you open My Documents, when you open a sub-folder, and when you are on Desktop.

CREATING A NEW FOLDER USING MY DOCUMENTS

❑ Click on Start. The Start Menu appears.

❑ Click on My Documents. The My Documents window appears.

❑ Click on Make a New Folder which appears in the left-hand column. The new folder appears on the screen at the bottom of the list of files and folders.

❑ Type a name in the highlighted box to rename the new folder.

❑ Click on a blank spot on the screen. The new folder appears with its new name. To place the new folder in another location, follow the instructions for moving files or folders.

❑ Exit by clicking on the Exit Button in the upper right-hand corner.

CREATING A NEW FOLDER WHILE IN A SUB-FOLDER

❑ Open a sub-folder. Do not open any file in the sub-folder.

❑ Right click on any blank space in the window. A drop-down menu appears.

❑ Click on New. Another drop-down menu appears.

❑ Click on Folder. The new folder appears on the screen.

❑ Type a name in the highlighted box to rename the folder.

❑ Click on a blank spot on the screen. The new folder appears with its new name.

CREATING A NEW FOLDER ON DESKTOP

❑ Right click on any blank space on Desktop. A drop-down menu appears.

❑ Click on New. Another drop-down menu appears.

❏   Click on Folder. The new folder appears on Desktop.

❏   Type a name in the highlighted box to rename the folder.

❏   Click on a blank spot on the screen. The new folder appears with its new name.

SHORTCUTS - LIKE USING A MIX

The icons that appear on your Desktop which have arrows in the left-hand corner are shortcuts for opening programs, folders or files. Instead of using the Start Menu to find and open a program, double click on the appropriate icon. The program, folder, or file is automatically opened. Add shortcuts to your Desktop for programs, folders, or files that you use frequently.

CREATING A SHORTCUT WHILE ON DESKTOP

❑   Right click on Desktop. A drop-down menu appears.

❑   Click on New. A drop-down menu appears.

❑   Click on Shortcut. The Create Shortcut dialog box appears.

❑   Click on Browse. The Browse for Folder scroll box appears.

❑   Scroll to find the folder or file for which you want to make a shortcut. To see files located within folders, click on the plus symbols to the left of the folders.

❑   Click on the appropriate file or folder but do not open it.

❑   Click on OK. The Create Shortcut Dialog Box appears. The name of the file or folder for which you want to create a shortcut appears in the "Type the location of the item:" box.

❑   Click on Next. The Select a Title for the Program dialog box appears. If you want to rename the shortcut, type in a new name.

❑   Click on Finish. The icon appears on Desktop.

CREATING A SHORTCUT WHILE IN MY DOCUMENTS

❑   Click on Start on the Taskbar. The Start Menu appears.

❑   Click on My Documents. The My Documents window appears.

❑   Right click on the folder or file for which you wish to create a shortcut. Do not open it. A drop-down menu appears.

❑   Click on Create Shortcut. The new shortcut appears at the bottom of the list of folders and files.

❑   Right click on the shortcut. A drop-down menu appears.

❑   Click on Send To. A drop-down menu appears.

❑   Click on Desktop. The shortcut appears on Desktop.

RENAMING A SHORTCUT ICON

❑ Right click on the shortcut icon. A drop-down menu appears.

❑ Click on Rename. The name of the shortcut icon is highlighted.

❑ Press Backspace on the keyboard. The name of the shortcut disappears.

❑ Type the new name in the empty box.

❑ Click on a blank space on Desktop.

DELETING A SHORTCUT ICON

When you delete a shortcut icon, only the icon is deleted. The program, folder, or file is not deleted. The program, folder or file must be deleted separately.

❑ Right click on the shortcut icon. A drop-down box appears.

❑ Click on Delete. The Confirm Delete box appears.

❑ Click on Yes. The shortcut icon is removed from the screen.

ADDING A SHORTCUT TO THE START MENU

A shortcut icon can be added to the left-hand column of the Start Menu for any program.

❑ Right click on any program icon on Desktop, in My Computer or in Windows Explorer. A drop-down menu appears.

❑ Click on Print to Start menu. The icon for the program appears in the left-hand column of the Start Menu.

REMOVING A SHORTCUT FROM THE START MENU

❑ Right click on any program icon which you have installed in the left-hand column of the Start Menu. A drop-down menu appears.

❑ Click on Unpin from Start menu. The shortcut icon is removed from the screen.

USING FLOPPY DISKS - LIKE FILLING YOUR FREEZER

If you are running out of space on your computer, you can store files on floppy disks, delete them from your hard disk, and restore them when you want to use them. It is a good idea to make several copies.

Floppy disks must be formatted before they can be used.   Disks that have already been formatted are readily available. Buy them and you won't have to learn how to format.

COPYING TO A FLOPPY DISK USING THE SEND TO MENU

❑   Insert a floppy disk into the floppy disk drive.

❑   Right click on the file or folder that you want to copy. Do not open it. If you select a folder, everything in the folder will be copied.   A drop-down menu appears.

❑   Click on Send to. A destination window appears.

❑   Click on 3 1/2 Floppy (A:). A Copying window appears, showing the progress of the transfer.

NOT ENOUGH ROOM ON THE DISK?

If there is not enough room on the floppy disk for the folders or files that you are copying, a message box appears stating that the disk is full. To continue, insert another floppy disk into the floppy disk drive and click Retry. If you do not want to continue, click Cancel.

VIEWING CONTENTS OF A FLOPPY DISK

❑   Insert a floppy disk into floppy disk drive.

❑   Click on Start. The Start Menu appears.

❑   Click on My Computer. The My Computer window appears.

❑   Double click on 3 1/2 Floppy (A:). The contents of the floppy disk appear on the screen.

❑   Double click on folders or files to view contents.

❑   Exit by clicking on Exit Button in the upper right-hand corner.

COPYING FILES FROM FLOPPY DISKS BACK TO THE HARD DISK

❑ Insert a floppy disk into the floppy disk drive.

❑ Click on Start. The Start Menu appears.

❑ Click on My Computer. The My Computer window appears.

❑ Double click on 3 1/2 Floppy (A:). The contents of the floppy disk appear on the screen.

❑ Click on folders until the file or folder you want to copy appears on the screen. If you select a folder, all the files and subfolders contained in it will be copied . Do not open the file or folder.

❑ Click on "Copy this folder" or "Copy this file" which appears in the left-hand window. The Copy Items dialog box appears.

❑ Click on the appropriate folders until you reach the folder where you want to copy the file or folder. Do not open it.

❑ Click on Copy. The Copying window showing progress of the transfer appears.

DELETING FILES OR FOLDERS ON A FLOPPY DISK

Files deleted from floppy disks do not go to the Recycle Bin. If a file is deleted from a floppy disk, the deletion is permanent.

❑ Insert a floppy disk into the floppy disk drive.

❑ Click on Start. The Start Menu appears.

❑ Click on My Computer. The My Computer window appears.

❑ Double click on 3 1/2 Floppy (A:). The contents of the floppy disk appear on the screen.

❑ Double click on folders or files until the one you want to delete appears on the screen. Do not open it.

❑ Right click on folder or file you want to delete. A drop-down menu appears.

❑ Click on Delete. The Confirm File Delete message appears.

❑ Click on Yes. Deleting progress message appears.

❑ Exit by clicking on Exit Button in the upper right-hand corner.

CHECKING AVAILABLE SPACE ON A FLOPPY DISK

❑   Insert the floppy disk into the floppy disk drive.

❑   Click on Start. The Start Menu appears.

❑   Click on My Computer. The My Computer window appears.

❑   Right click on 3 1/2 Floppy (A:). A drop-down menu appears.

❑   Click on Properties. Information on the capacity of the disk, the bytes used, and the free space available appears.

❑   Exit by clicking on Exit Button in the upper right-hand corner.

YOUR CD BURNER – NO POTHOLDER NECESSARY!

Many new computers come with a CD burner rather than a floppy disk drive. Learning how to backup with a CD is a little more complicated than learning to use floppy disks. Backing up files on a CD is much faster than copying them to a floppy disk. A CD can hold much more data than a floppy disk. You can store pictures and music as well as text on a CD.

The instructions which follow apply to computers which have Windows XP, a CD burner, and Roxio Easy CD and DVD Creator 6 or a later version. A CD must be formatted before files can be burned on to it. Roxio Easy CD and DVD Creator formats the CD automatically as part of the process.

THE TWO TYPES OF CDS

- **CD-R** - a CD on which you only copy material. You can override a file with a newer version of a file with the same name. If you delete a file, it is removed, but the space that it took on the CD cannot be reused.

- **CD-RW** - a CD on which you can copy material. The material on a CD-RW can be completely erased. New material can be added at any time.

COPYING FILES AND FOLDERS FROM THE HARD DISK TO A BLANK CD

Copying files and folders to a CD is a two step process. The first step requires that the files and folders be copied to a holding file. At this stage, files and folders that have been copied to the holding file can still be deleted because they have not yet been transferred to the CD. The second step involves the actual transfer or "burning."

❑   Click on Start. The Start Menu appears.

❑   Click on All Programs. A drop-down menu appears.

❑   Click on Roxio Easy CD and DVD Creator. A drop-down menu appears.

❑   Click on Drag-to-Disc. The Roxio Drag-to-Disc icon appears on Desktop.

❑   Click on the Menu Button on the Roxio Drag-to-Disc icon. A drop-down menu appears.

❑   Click on Keep in Front. This keeps the Roxio Drag-to-Disc icon visible when you open other windows.

EJECT SETTINGS

Roxio Easy CD and DVD Creator provides two options for formatting the CD. One option makes the CD readable on any CD drive. This process takes a little longer. The other option allows the CD to be read only on a computer running Drag-to Disc.

It is easier to select your option before you begin. You can change options with each CD.

❑ Click on the Menu Button on the Roxio Drag-to-Disc icon. A drop-down menu appears.

❑ Click on Settings. The Drag-to-Disc Settings dialog box appears.

❑ If you want the CD to be readable on any CD drive, place a check mark next to that option. If you leave the check box blank, the option that allows the CD to be read only on a computer running Drag-to-Disc will automatically take effect.

The Drag-to Disc Setting dialog box includes a check box asking if you want to show the Eject dialog box. If you have chosen your option, leave this check box blank. It makes ejecting the CD less confusing.

❑ Click on OK.

❑ Insert a blank CD into the CD drive.

❑ Locate the file or folder that you want to copy to the CD.

❑ Click on the file or folder to select it, but do not open it.

❑ Drag and drop the file or folder to the round disk on the Roxio icon on Desktop. The round disc on the icon will spin, indicating that it has received the file or folder.

DRAGGING AND DROPPING

To drag and drop a file, place the cursor on the title of the selected file. Keeping the left-hand button on the mouse depressed, drag the title of the file to the round disk on the Roxio icon. Release the button.

If you have inserted a blank CD-R

❑ The Drag-to-Disc Disc Preparation window appears with the message that the disk in Drive D: is being prepared. This takes only a few seconds.

If you have inserted a blank CD-RW

- ❑ The Drag-to-Disc Preparation Needed window appears with the message that this disk requires preparation that will take approximately 25 to 45 minutes.

- ❑ Click Yes.

- ❑ The Drag-to-Disc window appears with the message that the disk in Drive D: is being prepared. This will take 20 to 45 minutes. Please wait. A box showing the progress is displayed as is a record of time elapsed.

❑ Click on the Open Folder Button on the Roxio Drag-to-Disc icon. An icon for the file or folder which you have copied appears. Roxio Easy CD and DVD Creator has assigned a numerical name to the CD. It appears in the upper left-hand corner.

DELETING FILES AND FOLDERS

Because the files and folders which you have just copied have not yet been "burned" onto the CD, it is still possible to delete them.

❑ Right click on the file or folder to be deleted. A drop-down menu appears.

❑ Click on delete. The file is deleted.

❑ Continue to drag and drop as many files and folders as you want.

❑ Click on the Eject Button on the Roxio Drag-to-Disc icon. The CD will be ejected when the file or folder has been "burned."

NAMING THE CD

Roxio Easy CD and DVD Creator automatically assigns a numerical name to any blank CD which you insert in the CD drive. It is easy to rename the CD.

❑ Click on the Menu Button on the Roxio Drag-to-Disc icon. A drop-down menu appears.

❑ Click on Rename Disc. The Drag-to-Disc Rename Disc appears. The numerical name that Roxio Easy CD and DVD Creator assigned appears in the name box.

❑ Double click on the assigned name to highlight it.

❑ Click on the Backspace Key. The name box is empty.

❑ Enter the new name.

❑ Click on OK.

ADDING ADDITIONAL FILES AND FOLDERS TO A CD LATER

The procedure for adding files and folders to a CD which already contain files and folders is the same as that for starting with a blank CD.

COPYING FILES AND FOLDERS FROM A CD BACK TO THE HARD DISK

❑ Click on the CD icon which appears on under Devices with Removable Storage. The contents of the CD appear on the screen.

❑ Click on the Open Folder Button on the Roxio Drag-to-Disc icon. Icons for the files or folders which you have copied appear.

❑ Click on the file or folder to be copied. Do not open it.

❑ Click on "Copy this folder" or "Copy this file" which appears under File and Folder Tasks in the left-hand window. The Copy Items dialog box appears.

❑ Click on the appropriate folders until you reach the folder where you want to copy the file or folder. Do not open it.

❑ Click on Copy. The file is copied from the CD.

DELETING FILES AND FOLDERS FROM A CD-RW

❑ Click on My Computer on the Start Menu. The My Computer window appears on the screen.

❑ Click on the CD icon which appears under Devices with Removable Storage. The contents of the CD appear on the screen.

❑ Click on the file or folder to be deleted. Do not open it.

❑ Click on "Delete this folder" or "Delete this file" which appears under File and Folder Tasks in the left-hand window. The Confirm file or Folder Delete window appears.

❑ Click on Yes. The file or folder is deleted.

THE RECYCLE BIN – IT'S A GARBAGE DISPOSAL, TOO!

When you delete a file from your hard disk, it is not immediately removed from your computer. The file is automatically sent to the Recycle Bin which serves as a temporary storage facility. If you delete a file by mistake, the Recycle Bin gives you a second chance! A file sent to the Recycle Bin can be restored or, if you are sure, permanently deleted.

Files deleted from floppy disks are not sent to the Recycle Bin. When you delete a file from a floppy disk, it is deleted immediately.

The icon for the Recycle Bin is located on Desktop.

OPENING THE RECYCLE BIN

❑ Turn on your computer.

❑ Double click on the Recycle Bin icon on Desktop. The Recycle Bin window appears. The names of the files and folders that you have deleted appear.

VIEWING DETAILS OF ALL THE FILES AND FOLDERS IN THE RECYCLE BIN

❑ Click on the View Button on the Toolbar. It is the square white icon with small colored squares on it.

❑ Click on Details. The original location, date deleted, size, type of file, and date modified of all the files and folders in the Recycle Bin appear on the screen.

RESTORING FILES AND FOLDERS

When you restore a file, the file is automatically placed in the folder in which it was when it was deleted. When you restore a file that was stored in a deleted folder, the folder is automatically re-created and the restored file is automatically placed inside it. A file can also be restored and placed in a different folder.

RESTORING A SINGLE FILE OR FOLDER

❑ Click on the file or folder that you want to restore to select it. The selected file or folder is highlighted.

❑ Click on "Restore this item" in the top left-hand scroll box. The file is removed from the Recycle Bin and restored to its original location.

SELECT THE WRONG FILE?

If you select the wrong file to restore or change your mind about restoring it, right click on any blank space in the right-hand scroll box. A drop-down menu appears. Click on Refresh. The file is no longer selected.

RESTORING MORE THAN ONE FILE AT ONE TIME

❑ Hold down the Control Key on the keyboard while you click on each file that you want to restore. The selected files or folders are highlighted.

❑ Click on "Restore the selected items" in the top-left-hand scroll box. All the selected files are removed from the Recycle Bin and restored to their original locations.

RESTORING ALL THE FILES IN THE RECYCLE BIN AT ONE TIME

❑ Click on the Restore All Button in the left-hand scroll box. All the files are removed from the Recycle Bin and restored to their original locations.

RESTORING A FILE AND PLACING IT IN A DIFFERENT FOLDER

❑ Right Click on the file. A drop-down menu appears.

❑ Click on Cut. The file continues to appear on the Recycle Bin screen.

❑ Click on Folders in the Toolbar. A list of folders appears in the left-hand screen

❑ Click on the appropriate folder until the folder in which you want to insert the restored file appears.

❑ Right Click on the folder in which you want to insert the restored file. A drop-down menu appears.

❑ Click on Paste. The file is removed from the Recyle Bin and restored to its new location.

DELETING FILES

Permanently Deleting One File at a Time

❑ Right Click on the file that you want to delete. A drop-down menu appears.

❑ Click on Delete. The Confirm File Delete dialog box appears on the screen.

❑ Click on Yes. The file is permanently deleted.

Permanently Deleting All the Files at One Time

❑ Click on the Empty Recycle Bin Button in the left-hand scroll box. The Confirm File Multiple Delete dialog box appears on the screen.

❑ Click on Yes. The files are permanently deleted.

EXITING FROM THE RECYCLE BIN

❑ Exit by clicking the Exit Button in the upper right-hand corner.

CUSTOMIZING YOUR COMPUTER

Chapter 4

PERSONALIZING WINDOWS – BE YOUR OWN DESIGNER

All the elements that comprise Windows are presented in a preset format or theme. The theme which is installed when you purchased Windows XP is called Windows Classic. You can create a customized theme by changing various elements such as color, font, desktop background, sounds, icon size and arrangement, and screen saver.

If you make any changes to how any of Windows' elements are displayed, you automatically create a new theme. The new theme will automatically appear in a list with the preset theme. You can add or delete themes that you create.

Change themes as often as you wish. If you change your mind, you can always go back to the original settings.

DECORATING DESKTOP WITH WALLPAPER

Windows provides stock patterns and images which you can use to wallpaper Desktop. You can also use pictures that you have created with Paint, images that you have downloaded from the Web, or your own pictures that have been scanned into your computer.

❑ Right click on a blank space in Desktop. A drop-down menu appears.

❑ Click on Properties. The Display Properties dialog box appears.

❑ Click on the Desktop Tab. The Desktop dialog box appears.

❑ Scroll down the Background scroll box to see the choices available. The list includes stock patterns as well as any images which you have stored in the My Pictures folder.

❑ Click on your choice to select it. A picture of your selection is displayed on the monitor.

❑ Click on the Position Button scroll box. A drop-down menu appears which offers the following options for displaying wallpaper choices:

  • Tile: the chosen picture will be repeated enough times to fill the screen.

  • Stretch: the chosen picture will be stretched to cover the entire screen.

  • Center: the chosen picture is centered on the screen.

❑ Click on Stretch, Center or Tile in the Position scroll box. A preview of your selection will appear in the monitor.

SELECTING A DESKTOP COLOR

If you click on center, you have the option of selecting a border color.

❑ Click on the Color Button. A color selection box appears. You have two options:

    ❑ Click on one of the colors to select it.

    ❑ Click on Other at the bottom of the color selection box. A larger color selection box appears. Click on one of the colors to select it.

❑ Click on OK. The Display Properties dialog box appears.

❑ Continue making and previewing selections until you find one you like.

❑ Click on OK. You are returned to Desktop where the new wallpaper has been installed. If you change your mind, you can always do the whole process again and choose another image.

CHANGING THE COLORS OF WINDOWS' ELEMENTS

Windows allows you to change the colors and size of many elements. You can use pre-designed color schemes or design your own. If you tire of your choice, you can always pick another or go back to Windows Classic.

❑ Right click on a blank space in Desktop. A drop-down menu appears.

❑ Click on Properties. The Display Properties dialog box appears.

❑ Click on the Appearance tab. A model of Desktop with sample windows layered on it appears.

Changing Colors of Windows' Elements Using Pre-Selected Color Schemes

    ❑ Click on the down arrow in the Color scheme: box. A drop-down box listing all the pre-designed color schemes appears.

    ❑ Scroll through the drop-down box. Click on any scheme to highlight it. The name of the scheme will appear in the Color scheme: box. The color scheme will be displayed in the sample window.

    ❑ Click on OK. You are returned to Desktop. The new color scheme is installed.

Changing Colors and Size of Windows' Elements Using Your Own Color Scheme

    ❑ Click on the Advanced Button. A drop-down box listing Windows' elements appears.

❑   Scroll in the Item: box until the element you want to color appears. Click on the element to highlight it. The name of the element will appear in the Item: box.

Size, Color 1, and Color 2 boxes appear on the same line on the right. If any of these boxes are dim, the size and/or color of the dim box cannot be changed.

❑   Click on the up or down arrow to change the size of the selected element. The new size appears on the monitor.

❑   Click on each of the Color: boxes. A color selection box appears. You have two options:

❑   Click on one of the colors to select it.

❑   Click on Other at the bottom of the color selection box. A larger color selection box appears. Click on one of the colors to select it.

❑   Click on OK. The Display Properties dialog box appears.

❑   Click on OK. Your new scheme is installed and you are returned to Desktop.

CHANGING THE FONT SIZE

You can change the size of the text which appears on the Window elements.

❑   Right click on a blank space in Desktop. A drop-down menu appears.

❑   Click on Properties. The Display Properties dialog box appears.

❑   Click on the Appearance Tab. A model of Desktop with sample windows layered on it appears.

❑   Click on the arrow in the Font size box. Large, Normal, and Extra Large options appear.

❑   Click on your choice to highlight it. The selected size appears in the sample screen.

❑   Click on OK. The new font is installed. You are returned to Desktop.

ADDING YOUR OWN SCHEME TO THE THEME BOX

The Theme Box allows you to name and save the scheme you have created. This is useful if you want to change back and forth from one scheme to another.

❑   Right click on a blank space in Desktop. A drop-down menu appears.

❑   Click on Properties. The Display Properties dialog box appears.

❑   Click on the Themes Tab. The Themes dialog box appears.

❑ Click on the Theme scroll box until My Current Theme is displayed.

❑ Click on Save as. The Save as window appears.

❑ Rename the name which appears in the File Name: box by selecting the name that appears, clicking on the backspace key, and typing in the new name.

❑ Click on Save. The Display Properties dialog box appears. The new name appears in the Theme scroll box.

❑ Click on the Exit Button to exit.

DELETING YOUR OWN SCHEME FROM THE THEME BOX

❑ Click on the scheme that you have added to the Theme box list to highlight it. It will then appear in the "Scheme:" box.

❑ Click on Delete. The name of your scheme will be removed from the Theme box.

❑ Click on OK. You are returned to Desktop.

ARRANGING ICONS ON DESKTOP

You can arrange the icons that appear on Desktop. They can be lined up in columns, arranged by name, type, size, or date, or scattered randomly.

❑ Right Click on a blank space in Desktop. A drop-down menu appears.

❑ Click on Arrange Icons By. A drop-down menu appears with the following options:

  • Name, Size, Type, and Modified

    If you click any one of these, the icons will be lined up according to the option you select.

  • Auto Arrange

    If you check Auto Arrange, the icons will automatically be arranged in columns. No matter where on Desktop; you place a new icon, it will automatically be inserted into place.

    If Auto Arrange is not checked, icons can be moved randomly. Place the mouse pointer on the icon that you want to move. Keeping the left mouse button depressed, drag the icon to the place on Desktop where you want it to appear. Release the mouse button.

  • Align to Grid

    If you check Align to Grid, the icons which you have placed randomly are aligned in columns. The Align to Grid option only functions when Auto Arrange is not checked.

NO NEED TO STRAIN YOUR EYES

Windows allows you to permanently magnify all the text which Windows automatically places on the screen. There are also ways to temporarily increase the size of the text which you enter or download, making it easier to read.

INCREASING THE SIZE OF TEXT WHICH ALWAYS APPEARS ON THE SCREEN

The following procedure will increase the size of the text which automatically appears on the screen. It will not increase the size of text which you enter or download.

❏ Right click on a blank space on Desktop. A drop-down menu appears.

❏ Click on Properties. The Display Properties dialog box appears.

❏ Click on the Appearance Tab.

❏ Click on the arrow on the Font Size box. A drop-down menu appears.

❏ Click on the desired size.

❏ Click on OK. A message asking you to wait appears. The new text size appears on all applications.

CHANGING THE SIZE OF ICONS ON DESKTOP

❏ Right click on a blank space in Desktop. A drop-down menu appears.

❏ Click on Properties. The Display Properties dialog box appears.

❏ Click on the Appearance Tab. The Appearance dialog box appears.

❏ Click on the Effects Button. The Effects dialog box appears.

❏ Click on Use Large Icons. The checkmark appears.

❏ Click on OK. The Appearances dialog box appears.

❏ Click on OK. Desktop returns. Large icons are displayed.

THE ZOOM BUTTON IN MICROSOFT WORD

The Standard Word Toolbar includes a Zoom Button. It allows you to increase the size of the text on the screen as much as 500%. It is applicable only to the file which is currently open.

❏ Click on Start. The Start Menu appears.

❏ Click on Microsoft Word. The Microsoft Word window appears.

❑   Click on the down arrow on the Zoom Button on the Toolbar. A drop-down menu listing the possible degrees of magnification appears.

❑   Click on the desired degree. The size of the text on the screen changes.

THE MAGNIFYING GLASS

Some web sites include a magnifying glass icon on their toolbars. Clicking on the icon will enlarge the text on the screen temporarily.

THE SOUND SYSTEM – WHO NEEDS A HEARING AID?

Windows provides default sounds for certain program events. You can change the sound for all the program events that have sound associated with them. You can even add sound to other events for which Windows has not provided a default sound. If you change your mind, you can go back to the default settings. You can also adjust the volume of the sound system.

CUSTOMIZING THE SOUND SYSTEM

❑ Click on Start. The Start Menu appears.

❑ Click on Control Panel. The Control Panel window appears with a list of options.

❑ Click on Sounds, Speech, and Audio Devices under Pick a category. The Sounds, Speech, and Audio Devices window appears.

❑ Click on Change the sound scheme under Pick a task. The Sounds and Audio Device Properties dialog box appears.

❑ Click on the Sounds Tab. The Sounds scheme: scroll box and the Program events: scroll box appear.

❑ Click on the down arrow to view the list of events in the Program events: scroll box. An icon next to an event indicates that it has a default sound associated with it.

❑ Click on the event for which you want to change the sound or add sound to highlight it. The Sounds scheme: scroll box appears below.

❑ Click on the down arrow in the Sounds scheme: scroll box to view the sound choices.

❑ Click on your sound choice. The name of your sound choice appears in the Sound scheme: scroll box. If the program event for which you added sound did not previously have sound, a sound icon will now appear next to it. Continue adding sound to as many events as you want.

❑ Click on the Save As Button below the Sound scheme: scroll box. The Save Scheme As dialog box appears.

❑ Enter a name for the sound system you have created in the Save this sound scheme as: box.

❑ Click on OK which is below the Save Scheme As dialog box.

❑ Click on OK at the bottom of the screen. The Sounds, Speech, and Audio Devices window appears.

❑ Click on the Exit Button in the upper right-hand corner to exit.

REMOVING THE CUSTOMIZED SOUND SYSTEM

❑ Highlight the name of your customized sound scheme which appears in the Sound scheme scroll box.

❑ Click on the Delete Button. A message appears asking if you are sure that you want to remove the scheme.

❑ Click on Yes. The Sounds and Audio Device Properties dialog box appears.

❑ Click on the Sound scheme scroll box until Windows Default appears.

❑ Click on OK at the bottom of the screen. The Sounds, Speech, and Audio Devices window appears.

❑ Click on the Exit Button in the upper right-hand corner to exit.

ADJUSTING THE VOLUME

❑ Click on Start. The Start Menu appears.

❑ Click on Control Panel. The Control Panel window appears with a list of options.

❑ Click on Sounds, Speech, and Audio Devices under Pick a category. The Sounds, Speech, and Audio Devices window appears.

❑ Click on Change the sound scheme under Pick a task. The Sounds and Audio Device Properties dialog box appears.

❑ Click on the Volume Tab. The Device volume box appears in the center of the screen.

❑ Select the volume by depressing the left mouse button and gliding the arrow across the volume control. Release the mouse at the desired volume.

  To test the volume you selected, press and release the left mouse button on the arrow. The chosen volume is demonstrated.

❑ Click on OK. The Sounds, Speech, and Audio Devices window appears.

❑ Click on the Exit Button in the upper right-hand corner to exit.

THE SCREEN SAVER – PICK YOUR OWN

The telephone rings. You answer it. And it's a while before you get back to your computer. The window you were working on has disappeared. It has been replaced by the Screen Saver, a moving image that automatically appears on the screen to protect your monitor from damage which can occur when the same text or picture appears on the screen for a long period of time. As soon as you press any key on the keyboard, the Screen Saver disappears. Although a Screen Saver is already installed on your computer, Windows offers a collection of images from which you can choose. You can even use pictures you have downloaded or those you created with paint.

❑ Right click on a blank space in Desktop A drop-down menu appears.

❑ Click on Properties. The Display Properties dialog box appears.

❑ Click on the Screen Saver Tab. Below the picture of the monitor is a box labeled "Screen Saver."

❑ Click on the down arrow in the "Screen Saver" box. A drop-down list appears.

❑ Scroll down the list. When you click on an item, it appears in the display monitor.

❑ Click on Preview. The selected item will appear on the entire screen for a few minutes before returning to the display monitor.

❑ Scroll up or down in the Wait Scroll Box to select the time you want to elapse before the screen saver appears.

❑ Click on OK. The new screen saver is installed. You are returned to Desktop.

SETTING THE DATE AND TIME

The time is displayed in the right-had corner of the Taskbar. Your computer also includes a time zone setting that was probably set when your computer was installed. Because your computer records the date and time whenever you use a document, it is important that the date and time settings be accurate.

❏ Click on Start. The Start Menu appears.

❏ Click on Control Panel. The Control Panel window appears.

❏ Click on Date, Time, Language and Regional Options. The Date, Time, Language and Regional Options window appears.

SETTING THE TIME

❏ Click on Change the date and time. The Date and Time Properties dialog box appears.

❏ Select either the minutes or the hour in the box on the right underneath the clock by clicking. To move the time forward, click on the up arrow. To move the time back, click on the down arrow.

❏ If appropriate, select A.M. or P.M. and click to change.

❏ Click on Apply if you want to make other time/date changes. The new time is set.

❏ Click on OK when all changes have been made.

SETTING THE DATE

❏ To change the month, click on the scroll box on the left and click to highlight the correct month.

❏ Click on up or down in the year scroll box.

❏ Click on the correct date on the calendar.

❏ Click on Apply if you want to make other time/date changes. The new date is set.

❏ Click on OK when all the changes have been made.

CHANGING THE TIME ZONE

❏ Click on the Time Zone Tab.

❏ Click on the scroll box to select the correct time zone.

❏ Click on the Automatically Adjust Clock for Daylight Saving Changes check box.

❑ Click on Apply if you want to make other time/date changes. The new time zone is set.

❑ Click on OK when all changes have been made.

WORKING WITH PICTURES

Chapter 5

MY PICTURES – HELPS YOU ORGANIZE YOUR PHOTOS

My Pictures is a special sub-folder in the master My Documents folder. Whenever you download or scan in a picture or create one in Paint, it is automatically stored in the My Pictures folder. It provides links to help you organize your pictures including options for creating photo albums, slide shows, and filmstrips.

❑ Click on Start. The Start Menu appears. The icon for My Pictures appears in the right-hand column of the Start Menu.

❑ Click on My Pictures. The My Pictures window appears. It contains two screens. In the right is a list of all your picture files and folders. The left screen contains links to perform certain tasks and to other places.

IT'S YOUR CHOICE!

You can control the format in which the information appears on the right-hand screen. This is a particularly valuable option in My Pictures.

❑ Click on Views on the Toolbar. It is the square white icon with small colored squares on it. A drop-down menu appears with the following viewing options:

Filmstrip – Images are displayed as a filmstrip.
Thumbnails – Icons in boxes display up to four pictures in the folder or file.
Tiles – Icons are arranged alphabetically. Titles and information appear on the side.
Icon- Icons are arranged by categories with titles below.
List- Icons appear sideways with titles.
Detail- Icons appear in a list which includes size, type, and date modified.

❑ Click on any option. A black dot appears indicating your choice.
❑ You can change options by clicking on Views on the Toolbar and making another selection.

CREATING A PHOTO ALBUM

The Photo Album option is best for storing a small number of pictures.

❑ Click on Make a new folder which appears under File and Folder Tasks in the left-hand screen. A new folder icon appears as the last item in the right-hand screen.

Renaming the Folder

❑ Right click on the new folder. A drop-down menu appears.

❑ Click on Rename. The name New Folder is enclosed in a box.

❑ Type in the new name in the box. The name New Folder disappears and is replaced with the new name.

❑ Click on a blank space in the right-hand screen. The lines around the new folder disappear.

Putting Pictures in the Album

❑ Click on the icon for a picture which you want to include. Depressing the left mouse button, drag the icon to the new folder, placing it directly over the words "New Folder." The picture is now in the new folder. Continue adding pictures.

Put a "Cover" on the Album

You can distinguish one photo album from another by placing one of the images in the album on the icon which is displayed when you view your list of pictures in Thumbnail View.

❑ Right click on the new folder icon. A drop-down menu appears.

❑ Click on Properties. The New Folder Properties dialog box appears.

❑ Click on the Customize Tab. The contents of the new folder appear in the Preview box in the center of the screen.

❑ Scroll down the Use this folder type as a template scroll box which appears under What kind of folder do you want? until Photo Album (best for fewer files) appears in the scroll box.

❑ Click on Choose Picture under Folder pictures. The Browse window appears. Thumbnail images of all the pictures in the album appear on the screen.

❑ Click on the one which you want to appear on the icon in thumbnail view to select it.

❑ Click on Open. The image appears in the preview box.

❑ Click on OK. My Pictures appears. When the folders in My Pictures are displayed in thumbnail view, the icon for the photo album you created will include the image you selected.

VIEWING YOUR PICTURES AS A SLIDE SHOW

❏   Click on View as a slide show which appears under Picture Tasks in the left hand screen. A toolbar appears in the upper right-hand corner of the screen. If it does not appear automatically, move the cursor to the upper right-hand corner of the screen.

❏   Place the cursor on the arrows of the toolbar. Do not click. The function of each arrow is explained.

❏   Click on the arrows to display the pictures.

❏   Click on the Exit Button on the slide show tool bar to exit.

VIEWING YOUR PICTURES AS A FILMSTRIP

❏   Click on Views on the Tool Bar. A drop-down menu appears.

❏   Click on Filmstrip. The pictures are displayed like a filmstrip.

❏   Click on the right or left arrows to display the pictures.

INSERTING PICTURES INTO DOCUMENTS

Clip Art, pictures created in Paint, and photographs that have been scanned into the computer can easily be inserted into documents using Microsoft Word.

CLIP ART

Clip Art consists of pre-designed images. Unlike photographs, Clip Art has been drawn by computer. A collection of Clip Art is found in the Microsoft Office Design Gallery Live. New clips can be added from other Internet sites. Clips can be downloaded directly into a document or can be stored in Clip Organizer or in My Pictures.

❑ Click on Start on the Taskbar. The Start Menu appears.

❑ Position mouse on All Programs. A sub-menu appears.

❑ Glide the mouse across All Programs to Microsoft Word.

❑ Click on Microsoft Word. The Microsoft Word window appears.

❑ Double click on the White new folder icon to create a new file or double click on the yellow file folder to open an existing folder. Click until the file in which you want to make the insertion appears on the screen.

❑ Position the cursor where you want to insert the Clip Art.

❑ Click on Insert on the Menu Bar. A drop-down menu appears.

❑ Click on Picture. A drop-down menu appears.

❑ Click on Clip Art. The Insert Clip Art column appears on the right.

Inserting Clips from the Clip Organizer

Clips that you download from the Internet are stored in the Clip Organizer.

❑ Click on the Clip Organizer icon at the bottom of the right-hand corner. The Favorites-Microsoft Clip Organizer window appears. On the left of the window is a scroll box containing a list of categories for which Clip Art exits. The images for the category you select will appear in the center window.

❑ Click on the plus sign next to Downloaded Clips. Downloaded Clips expands into files displayed by broad categories.

❑ Click on any of the category files. The Clip Art contained in the file appears in the right-hand screen.

Viewing an Enlarged Image

The image must be displayed in Thumbnail form to view an enlarged picture.

- ❑ Click on the Thumbnail Button on the Toolbar. The images displayed in the category you chose are displayed in boxes.

- ❑ Place the cursor over the image which you want to enlarge. A box with a down arrow appears on the right of the image.

- ❑ Click on the down arrow. A drop-down menu appears.

- ❑ Click on Preview Properties. The Preview Properties dialog box appears with the enlarged image.

- ❑ Click on Close. The Favorites– Microsoft Clip Art Organizer window appears.

Inserting the Clip Art Into the Document From Clip Organizer

- ❑ Right click on the image. A drop-down menu appears.

- ❑ Click on Copy.

- ❑ Insert the cursor in the spot in the file where you want to insert the Click Art.

- ❑ Right click. A drop-down menu appears.

- ❑ Click on paste. The Click Art appears in the chosen spot.

Finding Clip Art Online

You must be connected to the Internet to access Clips Online.

- ❑ Click on Clips Online at the bottom of the column. The Microsoft Office Design Gallery Live appears. The following search boxes appear in the left-hand column:

  - • Search for: Enter keywords.
  - • Search in: Scroll down to select options.
  - • Results should be: Scroll down to select options.
  - • Order by: Scroll down to select options.

- ❑ Enter keywords and options.

- ❑ Click on Go. The appropriate clip art icons appear in the right-hand screen.

- ❑ Click on the left and right arrows in the upper-right hand corner to move from page to page to view all the choices.

❑ Click on any of the clip art icons to preview it.   The Microsoft Office Design Gallery Live Preview box appears. It contains an enlarged picture.

Inserting the Clip Art Directly into a Document

❑ Right click on the icon. A drop-down menu appears.

❑ Click on Copy.

❑ Click on the Exit Button in the right-hand corner of the Microsoft Office Design Gallery. Live Preview box.

❑ Click on the Exit Button in the right-hand corner of the Favorites – Microsoft Clip Organizer window.   You are returned to the document where you want to make the insertion.

❑ Insert the cursor in the spot where you want the clip art to appear.

❑ Click on the Paste Button. The clip art appears.

Inserting the Clip Art Directly Into the Clip Organizer

You do not have to put clips directly into a document. Clips can be downloaded from the Internet and stored in the Clip Organizer.

❑ Click on the icon to download the chosen clip art. Notice of the downloading process appears on the screen. The Clip Art is stored in Clip Organizer.

INSERTING PHOTOGRAPHS AND PICTURES CREATED IN PAINT

❑ Click on Start on the TaskBar. The Start Menu appears.

❑ Position mouse on Programs. A sub-menu appears.

❑ Glide the mouse across Programs and down to Microsoft Word.

❑ Click on Microsoft Word. The Microsoft word window appears.

❑ Double click on the White new folder icon to create a new file or double click on the yellow file folder to open an existing folder. Click until the file in which you want to make the insertion appears on the screen.

❑ Position the cursor where you want to insert the photograph.

❑ Click on Insert on the Menu Bar. A drop-down menu appears.

❑ Click on Picture. A drop-down menu appears.

❑ Click on From File. The Insert Picture dialog box appears.

❑ Scroll on the Look in: box until the My Pictures folder appears. The pictures in the file appear on the screen.

❑ Double click on the picture you want to insert. The picture appears in your document.

PAINT - LIKE TAKING A CAKE DECORATING COURSE

Windows provides the tools for you to create your own artwork or modify somebody else's. The blank screen is your canvas. Your limits are your imagination and the capabilities of your printer.

OPENING PAINT

❏ Click on Start, The Start Menu appears.

❏ Position mouse on All Programs. A sub-menu appears.

❏ Glide the mouse across All Programs to Accessories. A sub-menu appears.

❏ Locate Paint on the sub-menu. Glide the mouse across Accessories and down to Paint.

❏ Click on Paint. The Paint program appears.

THE PAINT WINDOW

The Toolbox

The Toolbox appears on the left of the screen. It contains the icons for Paint's drawing and editing tools. If you position the mouse on an icon, in a few seconds the function of that particular tool appears in a box.

To activate a tool, click on its icon.

The Color Box

The Color Box appears on the bottom left of the screen. On the left side of the Color Box the current foreground and background color selections are displayed.

To change the foreground color, click on a new color with the left mouse button. The new foreground color will be displayed in the Color Box.

To change the background color, click on a new color with the right mouse button. The new background color will be displayed in the Color Box.

The Drawing Area

The blank screen is the drawing area.

The Mouse Pointer Shapes

In Paint, the pointer that first appears on the screen is in the shape of a pencil.

The pointer changes shape as you utilize Paint's drawing and editing tools. In certain instances, the pointer will assume the shape of the icon of the tool you are using. In other cases, the pointer appears as crossed horizontal and perpendicular lines with a small circle where the lines intersect.

If you enter text in Paint, the pointer will be in the familiar I shape used in other programs.

THE PAINT HELP PROGRAM

Although you will only become skilled at using Paint through trial and error, the best place to begin is to use the Contents section of the Paint Help program. Paint's basic commands are explained in simple terms. The instructions for using the Help program follow, as do those for printing out the instructions for future reference.

❑ Click on Help on the Paint Menu Bar. A drop-down menu appears.

❑ Click on Help Topics. The Paint Help screen appears.

❑ Click on Contents tab. Two choices appear in the left-hand screen: Paint and Using the Help Viewer.

❑ Click on Paint. Sub-topics relating to the topic selected appear.

❑ Click on a sub-topic to select it. The instructions appear in the Paint Help box on the right of the screen.

PRINTING A HELP TOPIC

❑ Click on Options on the Menu Bar of Paint Help. A drop-down menu appears.

❑ Click on Print. The Print dialog box appears.

❑ Click on OK. The file is printed. The screen returns to Paint Help box.

Printing All the Sub-Menus of a Paint Help Topic at One Time

Instead of printing each sub-menu individually, all the sub-menus for any one item listed in the Contents section of Help Topics: Paint Help can be printed at one time.

❑ Click on a book icon to select it.

❑ Click on Options. A drop-down menu appears.

❑ Click on Print. The Print Topics dialog box appears.

❏ Click on the circle "Print the selected heading and all sub-topics".

❏ Click on OK. All the sub-menus for the icon you selected will be printed. The Paint Help box for the last sub-menu printed appears.

❏ Click on Help Topics on the Menu Bar of Paint Help box to return to the Help Topics: Paint Help window.

❏ Continue selecting instructions.

❏ To exit, click on the exit button that appears in the upper right-hand corner of the Help topics: Paint Help window. The Paint window appears.

WATCH OUT IF YOU CHANGED THE SIZE OF YOUR PICTURE!

If you changed the size of your picture by clicking on Attributes or Stretch and Skew on the Image Menu, the screen size that you entered will be applicable to the next picture you create. To correct this, when you begin a new picture click on Attributes on the Image Menu, click the Default Button, and then click OK. The size of the screen will be reset to the default setting for your next picture.

SAVING PAINT FILES

Because it is a good idea to keep all your Paint and picture files in one folder, Windows XP has created a "My Pictures" folder. The "My Pictures" folder is located as a sub-folder in the "My Documents" folder.

❏ Click on File on the Menu Bar. A drop-down menu appears.

❏ Click on Save As. The Save As dialog box appears.

❏ Type the name you are assigning to the file in the "File Name:" box.

❏ Do not change what appears in the "Save as type:" box.

❏ If My Pictures does not appear in the "Save in:" box at the top of the screen, click on "My Documents" which appears in the left-hand column. A list of sub-folders appears on the screen.

❏ Click on My Pictures until it appears in the "Save in:" box.

❏ Click on Save. You are returned to Paint and the file that you have just saved.

If you make additional changes, save them by clicking on save in the File Command drop-down menu.

❑ To exit from Paint, click on the Exit button in the upper right-hand corner.

REOPENING PAINT FILES

❑ Click on Start. The Start Menu appears.

❑ Position mouse on All Programs. A sub-menu appears.

❑ Glide the mouse across All Programs to Accessories. A sub-menu appears.

❑ Locate Paint on the sub-menu. Glide the mouse across Accessories and down to Paint.

❑ Click on Paint. The Paint program appears.

❑ Click on File. A drop-down menu appears.

❑ Click on Open. The Open window appears. Copies of the pictures in My Pictures file appear on the screen.

❑ Scroll down to the appropriate picture.

❑ Double click on the picture to open it.

ADDRESS BOOK

Chapter 6

ADDRESS BOOK

Windows provides you with a program to create an address book. Although the program has many features to create an address book applicable to business and more complicated uses, the instructions below are for creating a personal address book. You can add birthdays, anniversaries, children, and anything else you want to remember.

- ❑ Click on Start. The Start Menu appears.

- ❑ Click on All Programs. A sub-menu appears.

- ❑ Click on Accessories. A sub-menu appears.

- ❑ Click on Address Book. The Address Book – Main Identity window appears.

TYPING IN AN ENTRY

- ❑ Click on New on the Toolbar. A drop-down menu appears.

- ❑ Click on New Contact. The Properties dialog box appears. The Name Tab is on top.

- ❑ Enter the appropriate information. The name that you enter will automatically appear in the display box.

- ❑ Click on the Home Tab. Enter the appropriate address.

- ❑ Click on any of the other tabs for which you want to enter information. A dialog box appears for each tab. Enter the appropriate information.

- ❑ Click on OK. The Address Book – Main Identity window appears. The entry appears in the right-hand column.

- ❑ Click on the Exit Button in the upper right-hand corner to exit.

FINDING ENTRIES IN THE ADDRESS BOOK

- ❑ Click on the Find People Button on the Toolbar. The Find People dialog box appears.

- ❑ Enter the name in the Name: box. You do not have to type last name first.

- ❑ Click on Find Now. The name of the person you are looking for appears in the screen below.

- ❑ Click on the name. The Properties dialog box associated with that person appears.

EDITING ENTRIES

❑ Click on the Find People Button on the Toolbar. The Find People dialog box appears.

❑ Enter the name in the Name: box. You do not have to type last name first.

❑ Click on Find Now. The name of the person you are looking for appears in the screen below.

❑ Click on the Properties Button. The Properties dialog box associated with that person appears.

❑ Click on the appropriate tab associated with the information you want to edit or change.

❑ Click on OK. The Find People dialog box appears.

❑ Click on the Exit Button in the upper right-hand corner to exit.

ALPHABETIZING THE ENTRIES

❑ Double click on the column above the names. The list of names will be alphabetized in the Address Book-Main Identity window.

PRINTING THE ADDRESS BOOK

There are several printing options. You can print the entire list or selected names. You can include all the information or just the telephone numbers.

Printing All the Names

❑ Click on the Print Button on the Toolbar. The Print dialog box appears.

❑ Click on the All Button under Print Range.

Printing All the Information

❑ Click on the Memo Button under Print Style.

Printing Only the Names and Telephone Numbers

❑ Click on the Phone List Button under Print Style

❑ Click on the Number of copies scroll bar under Copies to select the number of copies to be printed.

❑ Click on the Print Button.

Printing Only Selected Names

❑ Click on the names which you want to include while holding down the Control Key. The selected names will be highlighted.

❑ Click on the Print Button on the Toolbar. The Print dialog box appears.

❑ Click on the Selection Button under Print Range.

Printing All the Information

❑ Click on the Memo Button under Print Style.

Printing Only the Names and Telephone Numbers

❑ Click on the Phone List Button under Print Style.

❑ Click on the Number of copies scroll bar under Copies to select the number of copies to be printed.

❑ Click on the Print Button.

COMPUTER CARE

Chapter 7

Housekeeping Chores - Even Computers Require Spring Cleaning

Just as your closets become cluttered, so do computers. There are several programs you can run periodically.

CHECKING FOR DISK ERRORS

❑   Click on Start. The Start Menu appears

❑   Click on My Computer. The My Computer window appears.

❑   Click on Local Disk (C:) to highlight it. Do not open it.

❑   Click on File on the Menu Bar. A drop-down menu appears.

❑   Click on Properties. The Local Disk (C:) box appears.

❑   Click on the Tools Tab.

❑   Click the Check Now Button in the Error-Checking box. The Check Disk Local Disk dialog box appears.

❑   Click on Automatically fix file systems errors.

❑   Click on Start. The Checking Local Disk (C:) dialog box appears.

You will probably get a message telling you that you must restart your computer in order to activate the checking. You have the option of turning off the computer immediately and restarting or having the checking take place the next time you turn on the computer.

❑   Click on Yes. You are returned to the Local Disk (C:) Properties dialog box.

❑   Click on the Exit Button in the upper right-hand corner.

DISK CLEANUP

If you are running out of disk space, run Disk Cleanup. It provides you with a list of temporary files that you can delete.

❑   Click on Start. The Start Menu appears.

❑   Click on All Programs. A sub-menu appears.

❑   Click on Accessories. A sub menu appears.

❑ Click on System Tools. A sub menu appears.

❑ Click on Disk Cleanup. The Disk Cleaning progress window flashes across the screen calculating the amount of space you are able to save. The Disk Cleanup for [C:] dialog box appears. It contains a list of categories of files that can be safely deleted.

❑ Click on the name of a category to highlight it. A description of the files appears in the Description box at the bottom of the window.

To View Files

❑ Click on a file to highlight it.

❑ Click on the View Files Button. A list of the highlighted files appears.

❑ Click on the Exit Button to return to the Disk Cleanup for [C:] dialog box.

❑ Click on the category of files that you want to delete to highlight it.

❑ Click on OK. Verification is requested about deleting the files.

❑ Click on Yes. The selected files are deleted. You are returned to Desktop.

DISK DEFRAGMENTATION

Disk defragmentation will rearrange programs on your hard disk to make your computer run faster. The disk defragmentation program tells you whether or not it is necessary to defragment your disk.

❑ Click on Start. The Start Menu appears.

❑ Click on All Programs. A sub-menu appears.

❑ Click on Accessories. A sub menu appears.

❑ Click on System Tools. A sub menu appears.

❑ Click on Disk Defragmenter. The Disk Defragmenter window appears.

❑ Click on the Analyze Button. Analysis is made, reporting whether or not you require the disk to be defragmented.

❑ Click on the Defragment Button, if defragmentation is necessary.

DESKTOP CLEANUP

Windows provides a Desktop Cleanup Wizard to remove desktop icons that have not been used for 60 days or more. You can choose whether or not you want to run the Desktop Cleanup Wizard automatically every two months. The icons which have been removed are stored in Unused Desktop Shortcuts which can be accessed

❑   Click on the Start Button. The Start Menu appears.

❑   Click on Control Panel. The Control Panel window appears.

❑   Click on Appearances and Themes. Options appear.

❑   Click on the Display icon under Pick a Control Panel icon. The Display Properties dialog box appears.

❑   Click on the Desktop Tab. The Desktop dialog box appears.

❑   Click on the Customize Desktop Button. The Desktop Cleanup dialog box appears.

❑   Click on the check box next to Run Desktop Cleanup Wizard every 60 days.

❑   Click on the check box next to Run Desktop Cleaning Wizard every 60 days to remove the check, if you not want this option.

❑   Click on OK. The Display Properties dialog box appears.

❑   Click on the Exit Button. You are returned to Control Panel.

RESTORING DESKTOP ICONS REMOVED BY THE DESKTOP CLEANUP WIZARD

❑   Click on the Unused Desktop icon which appears on Desktop. The Unused Desktop Shortcuts window appears. The deleted icons are listed.

❑   Right click on the icon to be restored. A drop-down menu appears.

❑   Click on Send To. A drop-down menu appears.

❑   Click on Desktop (create shortcut). The shortcut icon is restored to Desktop.

CHECKING YOUR COMPUTER'S SYSTEM

There are two Properties files. One gives you information on the available disk space. This is useful when you want to know if you have enough space to install a specific program.

The other Properties file tells you about your computer's resources. It has the answers to all the questions you are asked when you call a guru for help. For those users who want to know all the facts, look at it. Everybody else can skip it.

CHECKING DISK SPACE

❑ Click on Start. The Start Menu appears

❑ Click on My Computer. The My Computer window appears.

❑ Click on Local Disk [C:] to highlight it. Do not open it.

❑ Click on File on the Menu Bar. A drop-down menu appears.

❑ Click on Properties. The Local Disk [C:] box appears.

❑ Click on the General Tab. The screen will show how much space has been used and how much space is available.

❑ Click on OK to exit.

SYSTEMS PROPERTIES

❑ Click on Start. The Start Menu appears.

❑ Right Click on My Computer. A drop-down menu appears.

❑ Click on Properties. The Systems Properties Window appears.

❑ Click on the General Tab. Its lists the version of Windows you are using, your registration number, and your computer capacity.

❑ Click on OK to exit.

E-MAIL

Chapter 8

E-MAIL ADDRESSES AND SCREEN NAMES

MASTER SCREEN NAMES

When you set up an account with America Online (AOL), you are asked to assign yourself a screen name and password. The name that you select is permanent. It automatically becomes your e-mail address. You cannot change or delete it.

You may grant Master Screen Name status to two other screen names which have been assigned 18+ parental control, permitting them special rights to modify your account. Nevertheless, the ultimate responsibility for the account lies with the original Master Screen Name.

ADDITIONAL SCREEN NAMES

Although you have one permanent screen name, AOL permits you to have six other active names at the same time. Each of these names is assigned its own password and each acts as a separate screen name and E-mail address. Any of these six names can be deleted and replaced with another. A name can be restored after deletion so long as it does not remain deleted for longer than six months.

The use of other screen names affords you privacy and enables you to share your computer with other people. All billing is made to the master screen name.

CREATING ADDITIONAL SCREEN NAMES

❑ Click on Keyword on the AOL Menu Bar. A drop-down menu appears.

❑ Click on Go to Keyword. The Keyword dialog box appears.

❑ Type Screen Names in the text box. The AOL Screen Names window appears. A list of Screen Name Options appears in the upper right-hand corner.

❑ Click on Create a Screen Name. Create a Screen Name dialog box appears asking if the screen name is being created for a child.

❑ Click on No. (This is ok even if you are adding a name for a child.) The Creating a Screen Name dialog box appears.

❑ Click on Create Screen Name at the bottom of the window. Step 1 of 4: Choose a Screen Name dialog box appears. Read the instructions about choosing names.

❑ Enter the new screen name in the blank box.

❑ Click on Continue.

If the name you chose is already in use, a notice appears on the screen. Click on OK. You are returned to the previous screen to try again.

If the next name you chose is already in use, the Step 1 of 4: Choose Another Screen Name Dialog box appears. Two options are provided:

Suggest a Screen Name: allows you to let AOL suggest a screen name.

❑ Click on the circle next to Suggest a Screen Name: Place the cursor in the text box under Suggest a Screen Name: and enter a word that AOL will use to create a screen name for you. You can enter a word in each of the three boxes provided.

❑ Click on Continue. Step 1 of 4: Choose Another Screen Name dialog box appears containing a scroll box with a list of screen names from which to select.

❑ Click on one of the names to select it.

❑ Click on Continue.

Try Another Screen Name: allows you to try another name.

❑ Click on the circle next to Try Another Screen Name. Place the cursor in the text box under Try Another Screen Name: and enter a name.

❑ Click on Continue. If the name you choose is already in use, a notice appears on the screen. Click on OK. The Step 1of 4: Choose Another Screen Name dialog box appears again. Continue entering names until you find one that is not in use.

❑ When you have entered an acceptable name, the Step 2 of 4: Choose a Password dialog box appears with two blank boxes. Read the information concerning selection of a password. Type the new password in both boxes.

❑ Click on Continue. The Step 3 of 4: Select a Parental Controls Setting dialog box appears.

❑ Click on the appropriate circle.

❑ Click on Continue. If you have assigned General Access to the screen name, The Master Screen Name Status? dialog box appears. A dot appears next to No, Do Not Designate this Screen Name as a Master Screen Name. If you wish to grant Master Screen Name Status, click on Yes.

❑ Click Continue. The Step4 of 4: Confirm Your Settings dialog box appears.

❑ Click on Accept Controls. The AOL Screen Names dialog box appears. The new screen name appears in a box listing all your screen names.

❑   To exit click on the Exit Button in the upper right-hand corner.

USING MULTIPLE SCREEN NAMES

If you have created multiple screen names, when you sign on to AOL scroll down on the "Screen name" box, which appears in the AOL sign-on window to the name that you want to use. Enter the appropriate password. The e-mail messages that you send or receive will pertain only to the screen name that you entered when you signed on.

SWITCHING TO ANOTHER SCREEN NAME AFTER YOU HAVE SIGNED ON TO AOL

You can sign on to AOL under one screen name and switch to using another screen name without signing off.

❑   Click on Sign Off Button on the Menu Bar. A drop-down menu appears.

❑   Click on Switch Screen Name. Switch Screen Names dialog box appears.

❑   Click on the screen name to which you want to switch to highlight it.

❑   Click on Switch. The Switch Screen Name window appears.

❑   Click on OK. The Switch Screen Name Password dialog box appears.

❑   Enter the password.

❑   Click on OK. You are returned to the AOL Welcome window under the new screen name.

DELETING SCREEN NAMES

Be sure that you really want to delete the screen name. Although you are permitted to restore a screen name, if the screen name has been deleted for six months, it will not be possible to restore it.

❑   Click on Keyword on the AOL Menu Bar. A drop-down menu appears.

❑   Click on Go to Keyword. The Keyword dialog box appears.

❑   Type Screen Names in the text box. The AOL Screen Names window appears. A list of Screen Name Options appears in the upper right-hand corner.

❑   Click on Delete a Screen Name. A warning screen appears.

❑   Click on Continue. Delete a Screen Name dialog box appears.

❑   Click on the screen name that you want to delete to select it.

❑   Click on Delete. Notice is given that the name has been deleted.

❑ Click on OK. The AOL Screen Names window appears.

❑ To exit click on the Exit Button in the upper right-hand corner.

RESTORING SCREEN NAMES

A screen name that has been deleted within the past six months can be restored. The restored screen name will retain its original password.

❑ Click on Keyword on the AOL Menu Bar. A drop-down menu appears.

❑ Click on Go to Keyword. The Keyword dialog box appears.

❑ Type Screen Names in the text box. The AOL Screen Names window appears. A list of Screen Name Options appears in the upper right-hand corner.

❑ Click on Restore a Screen Name. The Recover Previous Screen Name dialog box appears. Deleted screen names appear in a scroll box.

❑ Click on name that you want to restore to highlight it.

❑ Click on Recover. Notice is given that the screen name has been recovered and the screen name list has been updated.

❑   Click on OK. You are returned to the AOL Screen Names window.

❑ To exit click on the Exit Button in the upper right-hand corner.

E-MAIL ADDRESS BOOK

AOL provides an address book in which you can insert e-mail addresses. It permanently stores the addresses and allows you to address an e-mail without retyping the address. You can use your address book to compile mailing lists to automatically send a particular e-mail to a pre-selected group of people.

It is not necessary to be logged on to insert, edit or delete names from your address book.

ADDING INDIVIDUAL NAMES TO YOUR ADDRESS BOOK

❑ Click on Mail on the AOL Menu Bar. A drop-down menu appears.

❑ Click on Address Book. The Address Book dialog box appears.

❑ Click on the Add Button on the bottom of the dialog box. The New Contact dialog box appears.

❑ Type in the name you want to enter in the empty text boxes provided at the top of the screen.

DON'T FORGET!

AOL automatically inserts the cursor in the "First Name:" box. You cannot type in any other blank box in the Address Book form until you first insert the cursor. To insert the cursor, position the mouse so that the "I" shaped pointer is in the blank box in which you want to type. Click on the mouse. A blinking perpendicular black line appears. As you type, the text appears to the left of the blinking line.

Assigning a Category to Those Listed in Your Address Book

AOL allows you to organize the names of those in your address book by category. To the right of the text boxes where you entered the first and last name is a category scroll box. You can assign one of the standard categories provided by AOL or add your own. It is not necessary to use this feature.

❑ Click on the Scroll Box until the appropriate category appears on the screen.

Below the text boxes in which you entered the name are three tabs: Contact, Home, Work, Details.

❑ Click on each tab and enter the appropriate information.

You can move back and forth from tab to tab. You can also correct typing mistakes. If you do not have all the information, you can return later and enter new data or make corrections.

❑ Click on Save. You are returned to the Address Book dialog box. The name that you just entered appears alphabetically in the scroll box. The information you entered appears in the scroll box on the right. Repeat the instructions to enter additional addresses.

❑ To exit click on the Exit Button in the upper right-hand corner of the Address Book dialog box.

MODIFYING ENTRIES IN YOUR ADDRESS BOOK

❑ Click on Mail on the AOL Menu Bar. A drop-down menu appears.

❑ Click on Address Book. The Address Book dialog box appears.

❑ Scroll to find name or mailing list you want to change and click on it to highlight it.

❑ Click on the Edit Button. The Address Card for the name you selected appears.

❑ Type in the desired changes.

❑ Click on Save. You are returned to the Address Book dialog box.

❑ To exit click on the Exit Button in the upper right-hand corner of the Address Book dialog box.

DELETING ENTRIES FROM YOUR ADDRESS BOOK

❑ Click on Mail on the AOL Menu Bar. A drop-down menu appears.

❑ Click on Address Book. The Address Book dialog box appears.

❑ Scroll to find the name or mailing list you want to delete and click on it to highlight it.

❑ Click on the Delete Button. A message appears asking if you are sure you want to delete the name.

❑ Click on Yes. A message appears stating that your address book is being updated.

❑ Click on OK. The Address Book dialog box appears on the screen. The selected name has been deleted.

❑ To exit click on the Exit Button in the upper right-hand corner of the Address Book dialog box.

INSERTING MAILING LISTS IN YOUR ADDRESS BOOK

Using your address book, you can create mailing lists by selecting those names that you want to include on the list.

❑ Click on Mail on the AOL Menu Bar. A drop-down menu appears.

❑ Click on Address Book. The Address Book dialog box appears.

❑ Click on the Add Group Button. The Manage Group dialog box appears.

❑ In Box 1 assign a name to the mailing list.

❑ In the left-hand scroll box in Box 2, click on the name of the person you want to include in the group list.

❑ Click on the Add Button. The name of the person you selected is removed from the left-hand box. It now appears in the box on the right. Continue this procedure until all the selections have been made.

To remove a name, click on the name in the box on the right. Click on the Remove Button. The name is removed from the right-hand box. It now appears in the box on the left.

❑ In Box 3, type the e-mail addresses of those you want to include in the mailing list. Separate each address with a comma.

❑ Click No in Box 4 unless you have established a group with whom you are sharing information.

❑ Click Save in Box 5. You are returned to the Address Book dialog box. The name of the group is alphabetized in the left-hand scroll box.

❑ To exit click on the Exit Button in the upper right-hand corner of the Address Book dialog box.

ADDING NAMES TO YOUR ADDRESS BOOK FROM AN E-MAIL

If you receive an e-mail from someone who is not in your address book, you can enter their address into your address book directly from the e-mail.

❑ Do not exit from the e-mail.   Click on the Add Address Button which appears on the right-hand side of the e-mail window. The Contact Details dialog box appears.

The e-mail address of the person who sent you the e-mail appears in the Screen Name text box, if the sender is a member of AOL. If the sender has a different Internet server, the e-mail address appears in the Other E-Mail text box. Enter the rest of the data in the same way that you normally add a name. You do not have to retype the name that appears in Screen Name or Other E-Mail.

❏ Click on Save. You are returned to the E-mail screen.

PRINTING YOUR ADDRESS BOOK

❏ Click on Mail on the AOL Menu Bar. A drop-down menu appears.

❏ Click on Address Book. The Address Book dialog box appears.

Printing the Entire Address Book

❏ Click on the Print Button. The Print dialog box appears.

❏ Click on Print All Contacts.

❏ Click on the appropriate circle under Format.

❏ Click OK. The Print screen appears.

❏ Click OK. The entire address book is printed. The Address Book dialog box appears.

Printing a Selected Group of Addresses

❏ Click on an established group to highlight.

❏ Click on the Print Button. The Print dialog box appears.

❏ Click on Print Selected Contacts.

❏ Click on the appropriate circle under Format.

❏ Click OK. The Print screen appears.

❏ Click OK. The group list is printed. The Address Book dialog box appears.

COMPOSING AND SENDING E-MAIL

Corresponding by e-mail eliminates stationery, envelopes, stamps, and trips to the post office. The same e-mail can be sent to one individual or to as many people as you like. You can send an e-mail as a carbon copy or even send it to someone without the recipient knowing anyone else got the same one!

An e-mail can be composed while you are online and sent immediately or stored for later delivery. You also have the option to write an e-mail while you are offline, edit it, store it, and send it later.

SENDING E-MAIL TO RECIPIENTS WHO ARE NOT IN YOUR ADDRESS BOOK

❑   Sign on to AOL.

❑   Click on Write on the Toolbar. A blank e-mail form appears.

❑   Type the address of the person to whom you are sending the e-mail in the "Send To:" box. If you are sending the e-mail to more than one recipient, separate each address with a comma.

DON'T FORGET!

AOL automatically inserts the cursor in the "Send To:" box. You cannot type in any other blank box in the e-mail form until you first insert the cursor. To insert the cursor, position the mouse so that the I shaped pointer is in the blank box in which you want to type. Click on the mouse. A blinking perpendicular black line appears. As you type, the text appears to the left of the blinking line.

❑   Type the subject of the e-mail in the "Subject:" box. What you type here will appear as the title of the e-mail when the recipient receives it. If you leave the "Subject:" box blank, when the recipient receives the e-mail it will be titled (no subject).

❑   Type your message in the large window. Your message can be as long or as short as you want.

❑   Click on the Send Now Button.   You will receive a message that your e-mail has been sent.

❑   Click on OK to exit.

SENDING E-MAIL TO RECIPIENTS WHO ARE LISTED IN YOUR ADDRESS BOOK

❑   Sign on to AOL.

❑   Click on Write on the Toolbar. A blank e-mail form appears.

❑ Click on the Address Book Button. The Address Book dialog box appears. Scroll on the list of addresses to find the appropriate address.

❑ Click on the appropriate address to select it.

❑ Click on the Send To Button at the bottom of the Address Book dialog box. A drop-down menu appears.

❑ Click on Send To. The recipient's address will automatically be placed in the "Send To:" box in the e-mail form.

❑ If you are sending the e-mail to multiple recipients, repeat the above steps for each recipient. AOL automatically inserts commas between each address.

❑ Type the subject of the e-mail in the "Subject:" box. What you type here will appear as the title of the e-mail when the recipient receives it. If you leave the "Subject:" box blank, when the recipient receives the e-mail it will be titled (no subject).

❑ Type your message in the large window. Your message can be as long or as short as you want.

❑ Click on the Send Now Button. You will receive a message that your e-mail has been sent.

❑ Click on OK to exit.

SENDING "CARBON" COPIES OF AN E-MAIL TO RECIPIENTS WHO ARE NOT IN YOUR ADDRESS BOOK

❑ Sign on to AOL.

❑ Click on Write on the Toolbar. A blank e-mail form appears.

❑ Type the address of the prime recipient to whom you are sending the e-mail in the " Send To:" box.

❑ Type the addresses of those to whom you are sending copies In the "Copy To:" box, separating each name with a comma. Do not leave blank spaces between names.

❑ Type the subject of the e-mail in the "Subject:" box. What you type here will appear as the title of the e-mail when the recipient receives it. If you leave the "Subject:" box blank, when the recipient receives the e-mail it will be titled (no subject).

❑ Type your message in the large window. Your message can be as long or as short as you want.

❑ Click on the Send Now Button. You will receive a message that your e-mail has been sent.

❑ Click on OK to exit.

❑ The names of both the prime recipient and those receiving "carbon" copies are included when the e-mail is received.

SENDING "CARBON" COPIES OF AN E-MAIL TO RECIPIENTS WHO ARE LISTED IN YOUR ADDRESS BOOK

❑ Sign on to AOL.

❑ Click on Write on the Toolbar. A blank e-mail form appears.

❑ Click on the Address Book Button. The Address Book dialog box appears. Scroll on the list of addresses to find the appropriate address.

❑ Click on the appropriate address to select it.

❑ Click on the Send To Button. A drop-down menu appears.

❑ Click on Send To. The prime recipient's address will automatically be placed in the "Send To:" box in the e-mail form.

❑ In the Address Book scroll and click to highlight the address of the person to whom you are sending a copy.

❑ Click on the Send To Button. A drop-down menu appears.

❑ Click on Copy To. The address of that person to whom you are sending a copy will automatically be placed in the "Copy TO:" box in the e-mail form.

❑ Repeat this procedure until all the names of those receiving copies are in the "Copy To:" box. If all the names are not in the Address Book, you can type names in manually, separating each name with a comma.

❑ Type the subject of the e-mail in the "Subject:" box. What you type here will appear as the title of the e-mail when the recipient receives it. If you leave the "Subject:" box blank, when the recipient receives the e-mail it will be titled (no subject).

❑ Type your message in the large window. Your message can be as long or as short as you want.

❑ Click on the Send Now Button. You will receive a message that your e-mail has been sent.

❑ Click on OK to exit.

❑ The names of both the prime recipient and those receiving "carbon" copies are included when the e-mail is received.

SENDING MULTIPLE COPIES OF E-MAILS THAT LOOK LIKE INDIVIDUAL MAILINGS

If you send an e-mail to multiple recipients, but do not want a recipient to know that anyone else has received the same e-mail, follow the instructions for sending "Carbon" copies but put parentheses around the list of recipients. Even if parentheses are added, each address must be separated by a comma.

If you use your Address Book, click on the Send To Button and then on Blind Copy. The parentheses and commas will be inserted automatically.

List one of the recipients as the prime recipient, even though all the recipients are equal. It is not necessary to put parentheses around the name of the prime recipient. When the e-mail is received, none of the recipients will know that it was sent to any one else.

If a recipient replies to your e-mail, your copy of the reply will include the name of all the recipients.

COMPOSING E-MAIL TO BE SENT LATER

Although you can compose e-mail to be sent later when you are connected to AOL, you do not have to be on line to compose e-mail to be sent later. If you want to compose an e-mail off line, click on AOL but do not sign in. The instructions are the same whether you are on line or not.

❑ Click on Write on the Toolbar. A blank e-mail form appears.

❑ Fill out the e-mail form in the same manner that you would if you were going to send the e-mail immediately.

❑ Click on the Send Later Button. A message appears stating that your mail has been saved for later delivery. The e-mail is stored in your Personal Filing Cabinet until you send it.

❑ Click on OK.

SENDING E-MAIL THAT WAS COMPOSED EARLIER

If you compose an e-mail off line, when you sign in you will receive a reminder that you have an unsent e-mail. Click on the appropriate boxes.

The instructions which follow are for sending e-mails composed earlier which you want to send while you are on line.

❑ Click on Mail on the Toolbar. A drop-down menu appears.

❑ Click on Mail Waiting to be Sent. The Mail Waiting to be Sent Later window with a list of unsent mail appears.

❑ Click on the appropriate e-mail to select it.

❑   Click on Send Now. You will receive a message that your e-mail has been sent.

❑   Click on OK.

RECEIVING, REPLYING, FORWARDING, PRINTING, AND DELETING E-MAIL

When you sign on to AOL the Mailbox icon on the Welcome screen and the Mailbox icon on the Toolbar will display a red flag on an open mailbox if you have unread mail.

After you have read your mail you can reply immediately, forward it, or print it. You can also save it in an Old Mail file for a limited period of time, keep it on the New Mail list as an unread e-mail, or delete it immediately.

READING AN E-MAIL

❑ Double click on the Mailbox icon on the Welcome screen or on the Toolbar. The New Mail window appears listing each unread e-mail and the subject, date sent, and screen name of the sender.

❑ Double click on the mail you wish to read to open it. The e-mail appears on the screen.

❑ If the entire e-mail message is not visible, click on the down arrow on the right-hand scroll bar to view whole text.

❑ Click on the Exit Button in the upper right-hand corner of the e-mail screen to return to the New Mail window. The name of the e-mail that you just read appears on the screen with a red checkmark indicating it has been read.

❑ To exit from the New Mail window, click on the Exit Button in the upper right-hand corner. The e-mail is sent to the Old Mail file where it will remain for several days after which AOL will automatically delete it.

ANSWERING AN E-MAIL IMMEDIATELY USING THE REPLY BUTTON

❑ Double click on the Mailbox icon on the Welcome screen or on the Toolbar. The New Mail window appears listing each unread e-mail and the subject, date sent, and screen name of the sender.

❑ Double click on the mail you wish to read to open it. The e-mail appears on the screen.

❑ Click on the Reply Button. (If you want to reply to the sender and to all the other recipients of the e-mail at the same time click the Reply All Button.) A new e-mail form appears. The recipient's name and the subject automatically appear in the "To:" and "Subject:" boxes.

❑ Type the message.

❑ Click on the Send Now Button. You will receive a message that your e-mail has been sent.

❑ Click on OK. The e-mail to which you were replying appears.

❑ Click on the Exit Button in the upper right-hand corner of the e-mail screen to return to the New Mail window. The name of the e-mail that you just read and replied to appears on the screen with a red checkmark indicating it has been read.

❑ To exit from the New Mail window, click on the Exit Button in the upper right-hand corner. The e-mail is sent to the Old Mail file where it will remain for several days after which AOL will automatically delete it.

INCLUDING QUOTES FROM AN E-MAIL IN YOUR REPLY

❑ Double click on the Mailbox icon on the Welcome screen or on the Toolbar. The New Mail window appears listing each unread e-mail and the subject, date sent, and screen name of the sender.

❑ Double click on the mail you wish to read to open it. The e-mail appears on the screen.

❑ Before you click on the Reply Button, highlight the text from the e-mail that you would like to include in your reply by inserting the cursor before the first word of the text to be included. Keeping the left mouse button depressed, glide the mouse over the text you want to include. Release the mouse.

❑ Click on the Reply Button or the Reply to All Button. A new e-mail form appears. The recipient's name and the subject automatically appear in the "To:" and "Subject:" boxes. The text that you highlighted appears in the message box. Included are date and time annotations.

❑ Type an additional message.

❑ Click on the Send Now Button. You will receive a message that your e-mail has been sent.

❑ Click on OK. The e-mail to which you were replying appears.

❑ Click on the Exit Button in the upper right-hand corner of the e-mail screen to return to the New Mail window. The name of the e-mail that you just read and replied to appears on the screen with a red checkmark indicating it has been read.

❑ To exit from the New Mail window, click on the Exit Button in the upper right-hand corner. The e-mail is sent to the Old Mail file where it will remain for several days after which AOL will automatically delete it.

FORWARDING AN E-MAIL

You can forward a copy of the e-mail to as many recipients as you want, using the Forward Button that appears to the right of the e-mail.

❑ Double click on the Mailbox icon on the Welcome screen or on the Toolbar. The New Mail window appears listing each unread e-mail and the subject, date sent, and screen name of the sender.

❑ Double click on the mail you wish to read to open it. The e-mail appears on the screen.

❑ Click on the Forward Button. A new e-mail form appears. The subject automatically appears in the "Subject:" box.

❑ Type the recipient's address in the "To:" box or use the Address Book to enter it.

❑ Click on the Send Now Button. You will receive a message that your e-mail has been sent.

❑ Click on OK. The original e-mail appears.

❑ Click on the Exit Button in the upper right-hand corner of the e-mail screen to return to the New Mail window. The name of the e-mail that you just read and forwarded appears on the screen with a red checkmark indicating it has been read.

❑ To exit from the New Mail window, click on the Exit Button in the upper right-hand corner. The e-mail is sent to the Old Mail file where it will remain for several days after which AOL will automatically delete it.

KEEPING AN E-MAIL ON THE NEW MAIL LIST AS AN UNREAD E-MAIL

The e-mail that you have read can be kept on the New Mail list. This is an easy way to save an e-mail that you want to reread or reply to later. It will remain on the New Mail list for a short time after which it will be automatically deleted.

❑ Double click on the Mailbox icon on the Welcome screen or on the Toolbar. The New Mail window appears listing each unread e-mail and the subject, date sent, and screen name of the sender.

❑ Double click on the mail you wish to read to open it. The e-mail appears on the screen.

❑ Click on the Exit Button in the upper right-hand corner of the e-mail screen to return to the New Mail window. The name of the e-mail that you just read appears on the screen with a red checkmark indicating it has been read.

❑ Click on the Keep As New Button on the bottom of the New Mail window. The red checkmark on the e-mail that you have just read is removed.

❑ To exit from the New Mail window, click on the Exit Button in the upper right-hand corner.

SAVING E-MAIL IN YOUR FILING CABINET

AOL allows you to save e-mail permanently either in an AOL folder or on your own computer. There is a limit to how much mail you can save in an AOL folder.

❑   Double click on the Mailbox icon on the Welcome screen or on the Toolbar. The New Mail window appears listing each unread e-mail and the subject, date sent, and screen name of the sender.

❑   Double click on the mail you wish to read to open it. The e-mail appears on the screen.

❑   Click on the Save Button. A drop-down menu appears listing two options:

On AOL – Saves the e-mail in an AOL folder.

❑   Click on On AOL. A message appears stating that the e-mail has been moved to an AOL folder.

❑   Click on OK. The e-mail appears on the screen.

On My PC – Saves the e-mail to your computer.

❑   Click on On My PC. A drop-down menu appears.

❑   Click on Saved on My PC. A message appears stating that the e-mail has been saved into the Saved On My PC Folder In Your Filing Cabinet.

❑   Click on OK. The e-mail appears on the screen.

❑   Click on the Exit Button in the upper right-hand corner of the e-mail screen to return to the New Mail window. The name of the e-mail that you just read appears on the screen with a red checkmark indicating it has been read.

❑   To exit from the New Mail window, click on the Exit Button in the upper right-hand corner.

OPENING YOUR FILING CABINET

❑   Click on Mail on the AOL Toolbar. A drop-down menu appears.

❑   Click on either on Saved on AOL or Saved on MY PC (Filing Cabinet). A double screen appears.

❑   Click on either Saved on AOL or Saved on My PC in the left-hand screen. The e-mails which you have saved appear in the right-hand screen.

❑   Double click on the appropriate e-mail to open it.

PRINTING AN E-MAIL

❑ Double click on the Mailbox icon on the Welcome screen or on the Toolbar. The New Mail window appears listing each unread e-mail and the subject, date sent, and screen name of the sender.

❑ Double click on the mail you wish to read to open it. The e-mail appears on the screen.

❑ Click on the Print Button in the right-hand column. The Print dialog box appears on the screen.

❑ Click on Print. The e-mail is printed. The e-mail remains on the screen.

❑ Click on the Exit Button in the upper right-hand corner of the e-mail screen to return to the New Mail window. The name of the e-mail that you just read appears on the screen with a red checkmark indicating it has been read.

❑ To exit from the New Mail window, click on the Exit Button in the upper right-hand corner. The e-mail is sent to the Old Mail file where it will remain for several days after which AOL will automatically delete it.

DELETING AN E-MAIL

An e-mail that is deleted is permanently removed after 24 hours. After that, you will never be able to retrieve it.

❑ Double click on the Mailbox icon on the Welcome screen or on the Toolbar. The New Mail window appears listing each unread e-mail and the subject, date sent, and screen name of the sender.

Deleting an E-mail That is Open

❑ Double click on the mail you wish to read to open it. The e-mail appears on the screen.

❑ Click on the Delete Button. A message appears asking you if you are sure.

❑ Click on Yes. The New Mail window appears. The e-mail that you deleted has been removed.

Deleting an Unopened E-Mail

❑ Click on the Delete Button. The E-mail is removed from the screen.

❑ Click on the Exit Button in the upper right-hand corner to exit from the New Mail window. The e-mail is sent to the Recently Deleted Mail file where it will remain for 24 hours after which AOL will automatically delete it.

CHECKING TO SEE IF AN E-MAIL WAS READ BY THE RECIPIENT

If an e-mail was sent to an AOL subscriber, you can check to see if and when the e-mail was read.

❑   Sign on to AOL.

❑   Click on Mail on the AOL Toolbar. A drop-down menu appears.

❑   Click on Sent Mail. The list of e-mails that you have sent appears.

❑   Click on the appropriate one to highlight it.

❑   Click on the Status Button. The Status window appears. The date that the e-mail was sent is listed.

   If the e-mail was read, the date and time when it was read appear.

   If the e-mail has not been read, a note indicating that it was not read appears.

❑   To exit click on the Exit Button in the upper right-hand corner of the Status window.

ATTACHING A DOCUMENT OR A PICTURE TO AN E-MAIL

A document is a text file. It can be in any form from a report to a letter. Any file that you have created with Microsoft Word is called a document. Pictures can be attached to a document.

❑ Sign on to AOL.

❑ Click on Write on the AOL Toolbar. A blank e-mail form appears.

❑ Enter the name of the recipient in the "Send To:" box manually or use the Address Book.

❑ Enter the title of the e-mail in the "Subject:" box.

❑ Type the e-mail message. If you prefer, you may type the message after you have made the attachment.

❑ Click on the Attach File Button on the bottom left side of the window. The Attach File(s) dialog box appears. "My Documents" appears in the Look In: Box at the top of the screen.

❑ Double click on the folder that contains the document that you want to attach to open it.

❑ Click on the name of the file that you want to send. Do not open it. The name of the file that you are going to attach appears in the File Name: Box.

❑ Click on the Open Button. You are returned to the e-mail form. The name of the file that you have attached appears on the bottom of the screen above the Attach File Button.

❑ Type in your e-mail message if you have not done so already.

❑ Click on Send Now. The "File Transfer" message appears. It records the progress of the transferring of the file. When the transfer is complete, it will indicate "File Done."

❑ Click on OK.

INSERTING A PICTURE INTO AN E-MAIL

Pictures can be inserted directly into e-mail. This is not the same process as attaching a picture to an e-mail. A picture that is inserted into an e-mail is visible when the recipient receives the e-mail. A picture that is attached to an e-mail must be downloaded before it can be viewed.

❑ Sign on to AOL.

❑ Click on Write on the AOL Toolbar. A blank e-mail appears.

❑ Type the name of the recipient in the "Send to:" box or enter using the Address Book.

❑ Type the title of the e-mail in the "Subject:" box.

❑ Text can be entered both before and after the picture is inserted.

❑ Click on the Insert a Picture Button on the e-mail Toolbar (the one that looks like a camera). The Pictures drop-down menu appears in the right-hand column.

❑ Click on Insert a Picture. The Insert Pictures in Mail window appears.

❑ Scroll down the box on the left until My Pictures appears.

❑ Click on My Pictures and any of the folders in My Pictures until the pictures appear on the right-hand screen.

❑ Click on the small box in the upper left-hand corner of the picture that you want to insert. A check mark appears in the box.

❑ Click on the Insert Button. The e-mail appears with the picture inserted.

❑ Additional text can be inserted.

❑ Click on Send Now. The Send Mail window appears indicating the progress appears. The message that the mail has been sent appears.

❑ Click on OK.

DOWNLOADING AND FINDING FILES THAT ARE ATTACHED TO E-MAIL

If you receive an e-mail with notification that a file has been attached, you must download the attached file first and then locate the downloaded file in order to read it. After you have located it, the downloaded file can be printed, renamed, or moved to a different directory.

SETTING DOWNLOAD PREFERENCES

AOL allows you to set your own download preferences.

❑ Sign on to AOL

❑ Click on File on the AOL Menu Bar. A drop-down menu appears.

❑ Click on Download Manager. The Download Manager window appears.

❑ Click on the Preferences Button. A list of options appear.

❑ Click on any option's button to activate it. A checkmark will appear next to those that are activated. It is highly recommended that you <u>do not</u> activate "Automatically Display Images After Downloading." If that option is <u>not</u> activated, the Download Confirmation dialog box appears when you download a picture which provides you with the information on where the picture was downloaded and a button to click to open the file. If you activate that option, the Download Confirmation dialog box will not appear and there will be no confirmation about the downloading process for pictures.

❑ Click on the Save Button. The Download Manager appears.

❑ Click on the Exit Button in the upper right-hand corner.

USING DOWNLOAD NOW

❑ Double click on the Mailbox icon on the Welcome screen or on the Toolbar. The New Mail window appears listing each unread e-mail and the subject, date sent, and screen name of the sender. If a file has been attached, the e-mail will have what looks like a double icon.

❑ Double click on the mail you want to read to open it. The e-mail appears on the screen.

❑ If a file has been attached to the e-mail message, the name of the attached file will appear above the row of buttons at the bottom of the window. The size of the file also appears. Make a note of the name of the attached file.

❏   Click on the Download Button. A drop-down menu appears asking you if you want to download now or later.

❏   Click on Download Now. A warning message appears.

❏   Click on Yes. The Download Manager dialog box appears.

❏   Click on the Save In: scroll box until the folder where you want to save the file to be downloaded appears.

❏   The file name appears in the Filename: box. If you have not done so already, make a note of it.

❏   Do not change information in the Save as Types: box.

❏   Click on Save. The File Transfer window appears showing the progress of the download. Notification is made of completion of the transfer.

❏   The Download Confirmation dialog box appears. It includes the name of the file, the location where it was downloaded, and current status.

❏   Click on one of the two options:

Open File – The downloaded file appears on the screen. When you close the downloaded file, you are returned to e-mail.

Find File –   A split screen appears. On the right is a list of all the files in the folder in which you saved the downloaded file. The downloaded file is highlighted. On the left are options which you can use with the downloaded file such as renaming, printing, etc.

❏   Exit by clicking on the exit button in the upper right hand corner of the window. The e-mail appears on the screen.

❏   Exit by clicking on the exit button in the upper right-hand corner of the window. The Online Mailbox window appears.

❏   Exit by clicking on the exit button in the upper right hand corner of the window.

USING DOWNLOAD LATER

❏   Click on the Download Button. A drop-down menu appears asking if you want to download now or later.

❏   Click on Download Later. Notification is given that the file has been added to your download later list.

❏   Click on OK. The e-mail window appears.

❑ Exit by clicking on the exit button in the upper right-hand corner of the window. The Online Mailbox window appears.

❑ Exit by clicking on the exit button in the upper right-hand corner of the window.

DOWNLOADING LATER

❑ Click on File on the AOL Menu Bar (You must be signed on to AOL). A drop-down menu appears.

❑ Click on Download Manager. The Download Manager window appears listing files to be downloaded.

❑ Click on file to be downloaded to highlight it.

❑ Click on the Download Button. A drop-down menu appears asking if you want to download now or later.

❑ Click on Download Now. A warning message appears.

❑ Click on Yes. The Download Manager dialog box appears.

❑ Click on the Save In: scroll box until the folder where you want to save the file to be downloaded appears.

❑ The file name appears in the "Filename:" box. If you have not already done so, make a note of it.

❑ Do not change information in "Save as types:" box.

❑ Click on Save. The File Transfer window appears showing the progress of the download. Notification is made of completion of transfer.

❑ The Download Confirmation dialog box appears. It includes the name of the file, the location where it was downloaded, and current status.

❑ Click on one of the two options:

   Open File – The downloaded file appears on the screen. When you close the downloaded file, you are returned to e-mail.

   Find File – A split screen appears. On the right is a list of all the files in the folder in which you saved the downloaded file. The downloaded file is highlighted. On the left are options which you can use with the downloaded file such as renaming, printing, etc.

❑ Exit by clicking on the exit button in the upper right hand corner of the window. The e-mail appears on the screen.

❑ Exit by clicking on the exit button in the upper right-hand corner of the window. The Online Mailbox window appears.

❑   Exit by clicking on the exit button in the upper right hand corner of the window.

LOCATING AND VIEWING DOWNLOADED FILES

Pictures that have been downloaded frequently have been compressed to facilitate transfer. Compressed files have .zip extensions. AOL automatically decompresses a file with a zip.extension as soon as you sign off AOL. Therefore, before you try to locate and view such a file, sign off AOL and then sign on again.

❑   Click on File on the AOL Menu Bar. A drop-down window appears.

❑   Click on Download Manager. The Download Manager window appears. It includes a list of downloaded files.

❑   Click on the appropriate file to select it.

❑   Click on the Open File Button. The downloaded file appears on the screen.

LEARNING ABOUT HYPERLINKS – WHY TYPE!

Hyperlinks are Internet addresses. There are two ways to tell someone about a particular site in an e-mail without typing the site's address. If you have an Internet site in your Favorite Places file, you can easily include the address or you can e-mail someone about a site while you are connected to it.

When the recipient receives the e-mail, the hyperlink appears in blue. The recipient can connect to the Internet site by clicking on the hyperlink.

INSERTING A HYPERLINK INTO AN E-MAIL FROM YOUR FAVORITE PLACES FILE

❏ Sign on to AOL.

❏ Click on Write on the Toolbar. A blank e-mail appears.

❏ Type the name of the recipient in the "Send to:" box or enter using the Address Book.

❏ Type the title of the e-mail in the "Subject:" box.

❏ Text can be entered both before and after the Hyperlink is inserted.

❏ Click on Favorites on the AOL Toolbar. A drop-down menu appears with a list of your favorite places.

❏ Click on the appropriate place to select it and, keeping the left mouse button depressed, drag the mouse across the title of the selection to the e-mail message box. A small white square appears on the screen as you drag the mouse. Release the mouse. The Hyperlink appears in blue in the e-mail message box.

❏ Additional hyperlinks can be inserted in the same e-mail.

❏ Click on Send Now. The message that the mail has been sent appears.

❏ Click on OK.

INSERTING A HYPERLINK INTO AN E-MAIL WHILE YOU ARE CONNECTED TO A WEB PAGE

❏ Be at the Web page that you want to insert as a Hyperlink into an e-mail.

❏ Click on the red Favorite Places Button on the Web page's Title Bar. A dialog box appears listing your options.

❑ Click on Insert in Mail. The e-mail form appears. The hyperlink has been inserted in the message box. The name of the hyperlink appears in the "Subject:" box.

❑ Type the name of the recipient in the "Send To:" box.

❑ Additional text can be inserted.

❑ Click on Send Now. The message that the mail has been sent appears.

❑ Click on OK.

ACCESSING A WEBSITE USING A HYPERLINK SENT IN AN E-MAIL

❑ Click on the hyperlink. You are automatically connected to the website.

CUTTING AND PASTING INSTEAD OF CLICKING TO ACCESS A WEBSITE

Only hyperlinks appear in colored type. You cannot access a website by clicking on a web address sent to you in an e-mail which does not appear in colored type. Frequently a web address is long and not easy to type. Typing can be avoided by employing the cut and paste technique.

❑ Highlight the web address by holding the left mouse down and dragging it across the address.

❑ Click on the Cut Icon on the Toolbar (the one that looks like a scissors). The address disappears from the e-mail.

❑ Insert the cursor in the text box on the Toolbar (the one where you normally type a web address).

❑ Click on the Paste Icon on the Toolbar (the one that looks like a clip board). The address appears in the text box.

❑ Click on Go. The website appears.

INSTANT MESSAGES AND THE BUDDY SYSTEM

The Buddy system allows you to communicate instantly with a friend while you are both online. To be part of the Buddy system, enter the screen names of those with whom you would like to be able to "chat" with on line. Whenever anyone on your list is online at the same time that you are, you are notified. You can customize your Buddy system to maintain your privacy and to control viewing and sound.

CREATING A BUDDY LIST GROUP

❑ Click on Community on the AOL Menu Bar. A drop-down menu appears.

❑ Click on Buddy List. The Buddy List window appears on the right of the screen displaying the names of Buddy List Groups. It lists pre-established categories for Buddies, Family and Co-Workers.

EVERY BUDDY MUST BE ASSIGNED TO A GROUP

You cannot just enter a name. Every name that you enter must be entered into a Buddy List Group. If the Buddy you want to enter does not belong in any of the pre-established categories, you can create an appropriate Buddy List Group.

❑ Click on the Setup Button at the bottom of the Buddy List window. The Buddy List Setup dialog box appears.

❑ Click on the Add Group Button. The Add New Group dialog box appears.

❑ Enter a group name in the text box.

❑ Click on Save. The Buddy List Setup dialog box appears. The name of the new group is displayed in the Buddy List Setup box and in the Buddy List box on the right.

❑ Click on the Exit Button in the upper right hand corner of the Buddy List Setup dialog box. The Buddy List box appears on the right.

CREATING A BUDDY LIST

❑ Click on Community on the AOL Menu Bar. A drop-down menu appears.

❑ Click on Buddy List. The Buddy List window appears on the right of the screen.

❑ Click on the Setup Button. The Buddy List Setup dialog box appears. Existing group names appear in the scroll box on the left.

- ❏ Click on the name of the group in the scroll box on the left in which you want to add a name to select it.

- ❏ Click on the Add Buddy Button. The Add New Buddy Dialog box appears.

- ❏ Enter the screen name of a buddy in the text box. Do not enter the Internet extension. (In other words, do not add @aol.com or any other extension).

- ❏ Click on Save. The new name appears under the name of the appropriate group in the left-hand scroll box.

   You can continue to add names to your Buddy List, repeating the above process. If you want to add names to different categories, scroll on the Buddy List Group Names box until the category you want is displayed.

- ❏ Click on the Exit Button in the upper right hand corner of the Buddy List Setup dialog box. The Buddy List box appears on the right.

SETTING PRIVACY AND BUDDY LIST PREFERENCES

- ❏ Click on Community on the AOL Menu Bar. A drop-down menu appears.

- ❏ Click on Buddy List. The Buddy List window appears on the right of the screen.

- ❏ Click on the Setup Button. The Buddy List Setup dialog box appears.

- ❏ Click on IM Settings. The Buddy List settings dialog box appears.

- ❏ Click on the Privacy and Security Tab.

- ❏ Click on the appropriate circles to select your preferences.

- ❏ Click on Save. The Buddy List Setup dialog box appears.

- ❏ To exit click on the Exist Button in the upper right-hand corner of the Buddy List Setup dialog box.

SENDING INSTANT MESSAGES WITHOUT THE BUDDY LIST

- ❏ Click on IM on the AOL Tool Bar. The Send Instant Message dialog box appears.

- ❏ Enter the screen name of the recipient in the "To:" box.

- ❏ Click on Send.

   If the recipient is not on line, a message appears on the screen. Click OK and exit from the Send Instant Message dialog box.

   If the recipient is on line, the Instant Message To: box appears at the top left-hand corner of the screen.

Your typed message appears after your screen name. The recipient's answer appears following yours. If you have activated sound, the sound will indicate to you that you have received an answer to your message.

Type additional messages in the bottom box, clicking on Send after each message. The new message will appear in the box as will the recipient's response.

❑ To exit click on the Exit Button in the upper right-hand corner.

SENDING INSTANT MESSAGES USING THE BUDDY LIST

❑ Click on the name of the buddy to whom you want to send an instant message to highlight it.

❑ Click on the Send IM Button at the bottom of the Buddy List window. The Instant Message dialog box appears. The name of the recipient appears in the "To:" box.

❑ Type the message in the message box.

❑ Click on Send.

If the recipient is on line, the Instant Message To: box appears at the top of the left-hand corner of the screen.

Your typed message appears after your screen name. The recipient's answer appears following yours. If you have activated sound, the sound will indicate to you that you have received an answer to your message.

Type additional messages in the bottom box, clicking on Send after each message. The new message will appear in the box as will the recipient's response.

❑ To exit click on the Exit Button in the upper right-hand corner.

THE INTERNET AND THE WEB

Chapter 9

GETTING STARTED WITH THE INTERNET

Just as highways connect one city to another, the Internet connects computers all over the world. The World Wide Web is the information stored on computers throughout the globe. Find the Web site where the information you seek is stored and you can view text, graphics, sound, and video. You may even be pointed to other sites.

THE NAVIGATION BAR

When you sign on to your Internet server, the Navigation Bar appears. It is the starting point for accessing the Web. It usually appears just above the blank screen. Only those functions which are applicable at the moment appear in bold. The Navigation Bar contains the following elements:

- Previous Button – The left-pointing arrow returns you to the previous page.

- Next Button – The right-pointing arrow takes you to the next page.

- Stop Button - Stops downloading of current page.

- Refresh Button - Downloads the current page again.

- Address Text Box – Empty text box in which to type a web site address.

- Go Button – Searches for the web site entered into the Address Text Box.

ACCESSING A WEB SITE BY TYPING THE ADDRESS

To access a Web site you must know the web address of the site to which you want to connect. If you know the address, all you have to do is type it in the right place, click, and the web site will appear on the screen.

❑ Insert the cursor in the Address Box. Enter the address.

❑ Click on Go. The blue triangle in the right-hand corner will spin until the site appears on the screen.

STATUS BAR

As the computer searches for the web site, a narrow bar appears at the bottom of the screen recording in blue how much of the site has been downloaded. When the bar is completely blue, the full site appears.

NAVIGATING A WEB SITE

Think of a web site as a magazine and the World Wide Web as a giant magazine rack. The home page is somewhat like the Title Page that contains the Table of Contents. Instead of holding the magazine in your hand and turning the pages or leafing back and forth from one section to another manually, you navigate the site's contents by clicking with the mouse

Web pages can be utterly confusing. To make matters worse, no two web pages are identical. Web pages do share some common elements. The name of the site appears on the left of the Title Bar. The Favorite Places Button appears on the right. Your Internet server's Navigation Bar appears above the Title Bar. It contains the Back Button (left-pointing arrow), the Forward Button (right-pointing arrow), a Refresh Button, and a Stop Button. Most web pages contain scroll boxes, graphics, and lists of options. Frequently there are text boxes with buttons next to them to click after you have entered the appropriate information.

UNDERLINED TEXT AS HYPERLINKS

Text that is underlined is a hyperlink to another web page. Clicking on the underlined text brings the page associated with the underlined text into view. When you click on a hyperlink, the blue triangle in the upper right-hand corner twirls. The triangle stops twirling when the new page has been fully downloaded.

GRAPHICS AS LINKS

To determine if a graphic is a link, position the mouse on the graphic. If the arrow is converted to the image of a hand, the graphic is a link. Click on the graphic. The hand changes into an hourglass that remains on the screen until the new page is downloaded.

OTHER TEXT AS LINKS

Text does not have to be underlined to be a link. To locate links position the mouse on lines of text. If the arrow is converted to the image of a hand, the text is a link. In some web pages the link appears as a dot next to the text.

SCROLL BOXES

In addition to being present on the borders of Web pages, scroll boxes appear frequently within web pages. Scroll down to see the contents. Click on an appropriate entry to highlight it. Double clicking on the highlighted entry will frequently connect you to a new page.

NAVIGATING FROM PAGE TO PAGE

To return to the previous page click on the arrow on the Navigation Bar that is pointing left.

To go to the next page click on the arrow on the Navigation Bar that is pointing right.

STOPPING DOWNLOADING OF THE CURRENT PAGE

To halt downloading before it is finished, click on the Stop Button on the Navigation Bar.

REFRESHING THE CURRENT PAGE

To reload the current page, click on the Refresh Button on the Navigation Bar.

GOOGLE – EVERYBODY'S FAVORITE SEARCH ENGINE

Think of a search engine as a library card catalog. Instead of opening a drawer to search for entries under subjects and subheadings, you enter keywords into a text box. The computer does the work. Google.com is the most popular search engine. With it you can perform basic or advanced web searches. You can search by broad categories or specific words. Its many features include image searches, discussion group postings, and updated news sources. You can even establish your own blog. A fee-based research service is also available. Google has many sophisticated features, but only those applicable to the beginning Google user are described here.

❑ Type Google.com in the text box of your Internet server.

❑ Click on Go. The Google home page appears on the screen. Tabs for the following options appear in a row below the title:

- Web - Used to perform basic and advanced searches.

- Images - Used to search for pictures.

- Groups - Used to access archives of discussion groups on every subject.

- News - Used to search and browse news sources. It is continuously updated.

- Froogle – Shopping information service.

- Local – Used to locate businesses and services by type and location.

- More – Used to access all the other Google services and tools.

PERFORMING A BASIC SEARCH

The Web tab is automatically highlighted when you log on to Google, The text box to perform basic searches appears on the screen.

❑ Type in one or more descriptive keywords in the text box. Google is not case sensitive. It searches on all the keywords which you enter in the order in which you type them. Google ignores common words such as "and." Google searches only the exact keyword. For example, if you type "horse," it will only search "horse," not "horses." Use the guidelines listed below:

- Make your keyword as specific as possible.

- Put the most pertinent word first.

- To tell Google not to ignore a common word, enter a blank space and a plus sign before the word.

- To tell Google to ignore a word, add a blank space followed by a minus sign before the word.

- Phrases of two or more words can be placed between quotation marks.

- Connect two searches with upper case OR (hotels Chicago OR Boston).

❑ Click on the Google Search Button below the text box. A list of web sites appears on the screen. Your query terms appear in bold type in each web site listed.

❑ Scroll down the list. If your query produces more than one page of sites, click on Next to see additional sites.

❑ Click on an entry to access its web site.

❑ Click on the Back Arrow on your Internet server to return to the list of sites.

Further Limiting Your Search

If your search produces too many irrelevant sites, you can further limit your search.

❑ Scroll to the bottom of the first page. A text box appears displaying the words you have entered for the search.

❑ Click on Search Within Results which appears next to the text box. A window appears containing an empty text box.

❑ Enter a specific term to further limit the search.

❑ Click on the Search Within Results Button. Any additional sites appear.

PERFORMING AN ADVANCED SEARCH

Using the Advanced Search option is not difficult. If you are looking for something specific such as the title of a book or a personal name, it is actually easier than doing a Basic Search.

❑ Click on Advanced Search which appears next to the text box. The Advanced Search window appears. The following text boxes appear offering specific choices:

- With all of the words.

- With the exact phrase.

- With at least one of the words.

- Without the words.

❑ Enter the words in the appropriate text box.

❑ Click on the Google Search Button on the right. A list of web sites appears on the screen. Your query terms appear in bold type in each web site listed.

❑ Scroll down the list. If your query produces more than one page of sites, click on Next to see additional sites.

❑ Click on a title to access its web site.

❑ Click on the Back Arrow on your Internet server to return to the list of sites.

FINDING PICTURES

Over 425 million pictures can be accessed using Google's Image feature.

❑ Click on the Image Tab which appears below the title on Google's home page. A text box appears.

❑ Enter the appropriate keyword in the text box.

❑ Click on the Google Search Button. The appropriate images are displayed.

DISCUSSION GROUPS

The Groups Tab gives you access to Google's Usenet, a data base of discussion groups covering a full range of topics dating from 1981. It is updated several times daily. You can post your own replies.

A newsgroup is comprised of a broad topic with subdivisions arranged hierarchically into increasingly narrow subtopics. The names of subtopics are separated by periods. Articles or postings (called "threads") are included in each newsgroup. They appear sequentially by posting date.

Postings to Google Groups are automatically submitted to a moderator for approval before being posted.

Brief instructions for accessing newsgroups are provided below, but a detailed explanation of Google Groups is beyond the scope of this manual. In order to fully understand the use of Google Groups it is highly recommended that you click on the Groups Help Button which is next to the Search Button on the screen which appears when you click on the Groups Tab.

Options for Accessing a Newsgroup

❑ Click on the Groups Tab which appears below the title on Google's home page. The Groups window appears listing groups by broad categories. You have the following options:

- Click on any of the broad categories.

  A screen with the first subtopics related to your chosen category appears. It includes the number of groups associated with each subtopic. Continue clicking on any subtopic until the window with threads appears.

- Click on Browse Complete List of Groups.

  The names of newsgroups appear in screens of 50 names each. Continue clicking on Next 50 Groups to see subsequent screens. Select a newsgroup and continue clicking until the window with threads appears.

- Type a keyword into the text box.

  ❑ Click on the Google Search Button. A list of newsgroups appears.

THE NEWS TAB

The News Tab allows you to search for continuously updated news sources.

❑ Click on the News Tab which appears below the title on Google's home page. The current top stories, arranged by categories, appear on the screen. A text box appears at the top of the screen.

❑ Enter the appropriate keywords into the text box to locate a particular news item.

❑ Click on the Search News Button. A list of articles appears.

FROOGLE

Froogle provides you with a way to search product information online. Included are price ranges, store-to-store comparison shopping, and ratings and reviews.

❑ Click on the Froogle Tab which appears below the title on Google's home page.

❑ Enter the name of the item in the text box. Use either the Basic Search or the Advanced Search. Pictures of all the available items for the name you submitted appear on the screen.

❑ Click on Compare Prices which appears below each item pictured. Comparative prices are not available for all items.

Froogle Help

Using Froogle is somewhat confusing. Google provides a Help Program.

❑ Click on Froogle Help which appears next to the text box on Google's home page.

❑ Click on Take the Tour to Learn More which appears in the left-hand column.

LOCATING BUSINESSES AND SERVICES

The Local Tab enables you to search for products and services by type and location.

❑ Click on the Local Tab which appears below the title on Google's home page.

❑ Enter the product or service in the What box.

❑ Enter the location in the where box.

BLOGGERS

A blog is a web site established by any individual to share their thoughts with others. Google provides a service which allows anyone to set up their own blog at no cost. A detailed explanation and instructions are provided.

❑ Click on the More Tab which appears below the title on Google's home page. The More, More, More page appears.

❑ Scroll down to Google Tools.

❑ Click on the Blogger icon. The Blogger window appears with the Blogger tutorial and instructions.

OTHER GOOGLE FEATURES

Google has many other specialized services.

❑   Click on the More Tab on Google's home page. Icons for all of Google's features appear on the screen.

❑   Click on any feature for a description.

FAVORITE PLACES

Favorite Places allows you to store web site addresses that you use frequently or want to return to some time in the future. If you enter the name of a site into your Favorite Places, you will not have to search for the site again or type in the address to connect to it.

ADDING A WEB SITE TO YOUR FAVORITE PLACES LIST

❑ The easiest way to enter a web site into your Favorite Places list is to be at that web site.

❑ Click on the red Favorite Places Button on the Title Bar of the web site. A dialog box appears listing your options.

❑ Click on Add to Favorites. The name of the site is automatically inserted into your Favorite Places list.

CONNECTING TO A WEB SITE USING YOUR FAVORITE PLACES LIST

❑ Sign on to your Internet server.

❑ Click on Favorites on the Toolbar. A scroll box appears on the left of the screen. It includes a list of the favorite places which you have entered.

❑ Scroll to find the favorite place you want to access.

❑ Double click on the name of the web site that you want to access. You are automatically connected to the chosen Web site.

LISTENING TO INTERNET RADIO STATIONS

If you have a sound card and speakers and are connected to the Internet, you can listen to radio stations from around the world. Because many radio stations transmit their programs on the Internet in a continuous flow called "streaming", you don't even have to download their radio programs to listen to them.

❑ Click on Start. The Start Menu appears.

❑ Click on All Programs. A sub-menu appears.

❑ Click on Accessories. A sub-menu appears.

❑ Click on Entertainment. A sub-menu appears.

❑ Click on Windows Media Player. WindowsMedia.com appears.

FINDING A RADIO STATION

There are several ways to find a radio station. You can select one from a featured list, or by genre, keyword, or zip code, or by performing a more detailed search.

❑ Click on Radio Tuner which appears in the left-hand column. A drop-down menu appears.

Featured Stations

On the left is a list of featured stations. Each has arrows next to its name. When you click on an arrow, a description of the station appears. On the right is an additional list of stations.

Searching by Genre, Keyword, or Zip Code

A search box to help find additional stations also appears in the right-hand column.

❑ Click on the arrow next to the search box. It is not necessary to type in a keyword. A dialog box appears.

❑ Scroll down the Browse by Genre box. A drop-down list of types of radio stations appears.

❑ Click on one of the station types listed in the Browse by Genre drop-down scroll box list. The station type appears in the Browse by Genre box. A list of the selected genre radio stations appears on the right.

To further define your search, enter a keyword in the Search Box and then click on the arrow and/or enter a U.S. zip code in the zip code box. The results of the search appear on the right.

Doing an Advanced Search

- ❑ Click on Use Advanced Search. The Advanced Search dialog box appears. It contains scroll boxes offering different searching options.

- ❑ Click on as many of the scroll boxes as you want to select the pertinent option. The option appears in the scroll box.

- ❑ Click on the Search arrow. A list of the appropriate stations appears in the right hand column.

PLAYING A RADIO STATION

- ❑ Click on the name of the station to which you want to listen. A drop-down menu appears.

- ❑ Click on the Visit Website to Play Button. The station website appears.

- ❑ Click on Play.

- ❑ Click on the Exit Button to exit.

CREATING A PRESET RADIO STATION LIST

- ❑ Click on the name of the station to which you want to listen. A drop-down menu appears.

- ❑ Click on the Visit Website to Play Button. The station website appears.

- ❑ Click on Add to My Stations Button. A notice that the station has been added appears.

OPENING A RADIO STATION FROM YOUR PRESET LIST

- ❑ Click on Radio Tuner which appears in the left-hand column of WindowsMedia.com. A drop-down menu appears.

- ❑ Click on My Stations. The list of your stations appears.

- ❑ Click on the name of the station to which you want to listen. A drop-down menu appears.

- ❑ Click on the Visit Website to Play Button. The station website appears.

INTERNET WHITE PAGES

You can find the address and telephone number for anyone listed in a telephone book in the U.S. It only takes a minute. There are many web sites on the Internet for accessing addresses. Two of the easiest are listed below.

AOL WHITE PAGES

❑ Sign on to AOL.

❑ Click on Community on the Toolbar. A drop-down menu appears.

❑ Click on White Pages. The AOL White Pages window appears.

❑ Enter the appropriate information in the text boxes. The only information that you must include is the last name.

❑ Click on Search. The search results appear.

❑ Scroll to see all the results, clicking on Next, if there are additional names to be displayed.

WHITE PAGES.COM

❑ Connect to the Internet

❑ Type Whitepages.com in the text box of your Internet server.

❑ Click on Go. The Whitepages.com page appears on the screen.

❑ Enter the appropriate information in the text boxes. The only information that you must include is the last name.

❑ Click on Search. The search results appear.

❑ Scroll to see all the results, clicking on Next, if there are additional names to be displayed.

If the name and address you want do not appear, follow the instructions on the screen to add additional information.

CHAT ROOMS

Chat rooms are sites devoted to specific subjects where AOL members can communicate instantly with all those connected to the chat room. AOL has two types of chat rooms. Both are open to all AOL members. Created by People Connection Chats are chat rooms that have been created and named by AOL. AOL Member Chats are chat rooms created by AOL members. If you participate in the conversation, what you write is viewed by all those present.

If any of the participants in a chat room has filled out the member profile option, you can access their profile to learn more about that person.

❑   Sign on to AOL.

❑   Click on People on the AOL Toolbar. The People Connection dialog box appears.

❑   Click on Chat Room Listings. The AOL Chat Room Listings window appears. On the left is a scroll box with the following two tabs above it: Created by People Connection Tab and Created by AOL Members Tab.

❑   Click on either the Created by People Connection Tab or the Created by AOL Members Tab. A scroll box contains a listing of all the categories associated with the chosen tab chat rooms appears on the left.

❑   Double click on the appropriate category in the left-hand scroll box to highlight it. A list of the names of all the chat rooms for that category and the number of people associated with each appears on the scroll box on the right.

❑   Click on the appropriate chat room in the right-hand scroll box to select it.

❑   Click on the Go Chat Button. The screen for the chat room you selected appears. On the left is a large discussion box in which the screen name and comments of the people "chatting" appear.

❑   Enter your comments in the small text box on the bottom left of the screen.

❑   Click on the Send Button. Your comments will appear in the discussion box.

❑   To exit click on the Exit Button in the upper right-hand corner of the chat room window.

LEARNING ABOUT THE PARTICIPANTS IN THE CHAT ROOM

A scroll box appears on the right of the chat room window listing the names of all those currently participating in the chat room.

❑ Double click on the screen name of a participant in the scroll box on the right. A dialog box for that screen name appears.

❑ Click on the circle next to Get Profile. If a profile is available, it appears on the screen. If a profile is not available, notification appears on the screen. Click on OK.

❑ To exit click on the Exit Button until you are returned to the chat room.

CHAT ROOM SMILEYS AND SHORTHAND

Chat room participants use special characters and abbreviations to express emotions. The following web site contains a master list of smileys:

http://members.aol.com/bearpage/smileys.htm

GLOSSARY

GLOSSARY

Attach - Send a file with an e-mail.

Backup - Make copies of files.

Baud - Speed at which data is transferred by modem over telephone lines.

Boot - Start the computer.

Browser - Program for reading information on the World Wide Web

Byte - Memory required to store one character of information.

CD-Rom - Portable disk on which computer data is stored. Most programs come on CD-Roms.

Chat - Communicate with people online with immediate feedback.

Cursor - Pointer used to indicate the insertion point.

Database - Collection of information stored on the computer and organized for easy access.

Desktop - Starting screen for Windows.

Dialog Box - Window with blanks to fill in or options to choose.

Download - Transfer information from one computer to another.

Drop-down Menu - List of options from which to choose.

E-Mail Address - Name assumed to receive or send e-mail. Includes screen name and Internet server.

File - Any amount of information stored together as a single entity.

Floppy Disk - Portable disk used to store copies of computer data.

Folder - Storage unit for one or more files.

FTP (File Transfer Protocol) - Way to transfer files from one computer to another over the Internet.

Hard Disk - Non-removable disk.

Home Page - First page of a web site.

Hyperlink - Link to move from one web page to another or to include a web site address in an E-Mail.

Icon - Symbol depicting a command.

Keyword - Descriptive word used to locate information.

Kilobyte - 1,024 bytes.

Log On - Connect to Internet server by typing screen name and password

Megabyte - 1,048,576 bytes.

Modem - Equipment through which computer receives data over telephone lines.

Newsgroups - Internet discussion groups devoted to particular subjects.

Online - Connected to another computer via a modem.

Random-Access Memory (RAM) - Temporary storage area for data used when running a program.

Screen Name - Name assumed to identify oneself on line.

Search Engines - Software used to search for information on the Web.

Smiley - Keyboard characters entered in a pattern to depict a particular emotion.

URL (Uniform Resource Locator) - Identifying address for a web site.

Web Site - Set of pages on the World Wide Web.

World Wide Web - Sets of interconnected multimedia documents on the Internet.

INDEX

-NOTES-

-NOTES-